Positive Thinking

Discover the Power of Positive
Thinking and Change Your
Mindset to Become an Optimist

Part of the **[Mind Hacks]** series

By **Hanif Raah**

Axiom Core Publishing

Table of Contents

Introduction – Why Should You Read This Book?

Is your glass half empty or half full?

This simple but age old question is a great reflection on your life as a whole and studies show that these very traits, of optimism and pessimism, even affect your health and well-being. Whatever your train of thought is at this very moment in time, it is changeable and the fact that you are reading this right now proves that you want to take those steps on the path to positivity and instill a positive thinking mindset.

This book contains proven steps and strategies on how to discover, understand and use the power of positive thinking and change your mindset to become an optimist. This is not all, you will learn to use this wonderful power to make your life better all round.

Everybody loves an optimist, a person who loves life, is always smiling and sees the good side in everything. You do, too. So, why can't you be that person yourself?

Positive thoughts make you walk tall, stay happy and strong in the face of adversity, see opportunities where others see only obstacles, and what is most important, be healthy. Having a positive mindset naturally draws people to you as there is a certain vibe about you, an aura that is almost magnetic and powerful.

To be able to use this power, you will need to work a little to activate it. The ability is there in every human being. However, in some it is dormant or buried deep inside and it requires awakening. While this may take some time, just understanding and acknowledging its powers can be quite a revelation for you.

Find out what fills you with negative thoughts and how this is silently poisoning your life, preventing you from achieving your full potential. Why it is so difficult to break away from negativity and how it takes root in your heart and mind, sapping your energy and happiness. Find out how to trigger the transitioning to a purposeful, prosperous, enriching and happy life by using positive thoughts.

Positive thinking will transform you into a better human being, better worker, happier person and definitely more successful in every aspect of your life. It will wipe out the signs of stress, keep the door open to happiness and inspire you to climb above disappointment and failure whenever you meet it.

Wouldn't it be wonderful to be able to harness the power of positive thinking in your life? This book will show you how to do just that. I hope you enjoy it!

Chapter 1: What Is Positive Thinking?

Positive thinking is all about seeing the bright side of things no matter what. In other words, teaching yourself to perceive things in a better light rather than worse, consciously. Why is this good? A positive person attracts positive things and hence, is able to live a better, fuller, healthier and most important of all happier life.

It is very important that you make up your mind to see the good, the silver lining, in every situation. Only when you master this art, you would be able to move through life (relatively) unscathed by the troubles it throws at you. As Abraham Lincoln said, *"We can complain because rose bushes have thorns, or rejoice because thorn bushes have roses."* It's just the way you look at it.

Positive thinking is always hoping that the best happens, but not blindly. You are aware that things could go wrong and of what could go wrong and you prepare yourself to prevent any mishaps. Whenever things do go wrong, instead of despair you see a new opportunity.

Why Thinking Positive Is Good For You?

First of all answer this question. If you had to choose, whom would you choose to be around – a gloomy person, who is whining about everything and everyone or a radiant person who loves everything and everybody?

A negative person would seem to be draining the energy out of you, tiring you mentally and emotionally while a radiant person would charge your mind and body. So, isn't a positive person better than a negative one to have around?

Other benefits of positive thinking are:

- **You think better and clearer** when you focus on the positive, because you see the positive. When a pessimist sees a door closing, you see an opportunity of finding another way.

- **You have more friends**. People like to hang around with you because you are fun, inspiring and happy. You make them feel good and your positive attitude rubs off on them.

- **You work better**. When your mind is filled with positive thoughts your mind functions better and is more productive. You work better and longer when you are happy than when you are depressed.

- **You are a better** friend, parent, spouse, child, or worker. When you are positive, you tend to be more empathic, kinder, more conscientious, and easier to talk to, and so on. In other words, being a positive person makes you a better person.

- **You are healthier**. Being positive keeps your stress levels down and keeps your body and mind protected from the side effects of stress– things like high blood pressure, heart problems, high cholesterol, risk of heart attack, gastric problems, memory loss, risk of diabetes and so many more.

- **You stay younger longer** – as a positive person you worry less, and are able to keep stress from building up enough to harm you. This means you counter all aging symptoms better – you look better, you feel better, you keep all age-related problems (cholesterol, heart problems, memory problems, at bay and hence you live longer.

As you can see, positive thinking means positive actions, and in turn it means leading a happier, healthier and fuller life.

Positive thinking will have you looking at every situation – even the worst ones – with a belief that some good will come out of it. It will sustain belief in yourself and others and will always work to find the most constructive course of action.

Who Are You? Are You A Positive or Negative Thinker?

There is one thing that you should know, i.e. there is no absolute reality; only perceived reality; and the way you perceive it influences the way you think, feel and act. That would explain why two people see the same thing and yet interpret it in totally different ways.

Referring back to "the glass half full or half empty". This is just one tiny example about how important is perspective in how you see the world around you. The way you see the world is determined by the way you look at yourself. This also determines the way you feel about yourself and others, as well as the way you tend to act in any given situation.

Hence, the first thing you should know really well is yourself. You will be surprised how little you know about yourself until you are really looking. Who are you? Put this question to yourself often and look for answers inside.

What you are looking for? You need to look inside and answer truthfully whether you are an optimist or a pessimist? Are you an extrovert or an introvert? Are you a leader or a follower? These are only a few questions that you need to answer about yourself. You also need to find out what type of personality you are.

Most people do not really need quizzes to tell them who they are. All you need is to take a long and deep look at yourself to understand why you react the way you react.

Once you start understanding yourself, a lot of things will fall into place. It is exceptionally useful to know yourself because this will explain to you why you behave the way you do, why you think the way you do and why you feel the way you do. This is important because only when you understand yourself you can accept yourself for who you are – and then, identify with clarity which areas are your strong points and which areas are your weak points.

You can then know where you need to improve yourself, where you need to let go of emotional baggage by forgiving yourself and others and how you can move on and forward. People who respond to stressful situations with anger, frustration, self-pity and depression – negative feelings and behavior - are actually saying that they are not happy with who they are. These reactions are more often than not caused by low self-esteem and low self-confidence.

What Is Low Self-Esteem? How Does It Kill Positive Thinking?

Did you know that every person is the result of *three perceptions* rolled into one? The first is who you think you are; the second is who you think others think you are; and the third is what others think you are. These three perceptions determine the way you behave and look at the world.

Sometimes, you pay too much attention to one facet and everything goes awry. The perceptions change and everything and everybody look ominous and forbidding. This is the time when you become unhappy. Unhappiness has a way of blocking the capacity to recognize or appreciate anything positive around you. At such times, you need to take a deep breath and analyze as objectively as you can the reason for your unhappiness.   What is the trigger? Ask yourself these two questions:

1) Am I really threatened by this particular situation?
2) If yes, do I have the means and/ or capability to handle the threat?

The level of stress is directly proportionate to the ability to resolve the situation. It is true that sometimes situations are indeed truly life threatening such as a terminal illness, natural calamities, sudden and total loss of income, life threats, accidents, physical attacks, etc. However, in many cases situations causing stress are just things perceived in negative light.

In real and life-threatening situations, stress is a positive sign as it sends out as "warning signals" or "alarms" that tell you to prepare yourself for what is to come. It tells you, "take action now and save yourself".

However, there would be many cases where stress is the result of our wrong perception of a given situation. In such cases, you would feel that you are the victim of a situation, where you cannot do anything to help yourself.

This is when you become unhappy, worried and stressed and when you are unhappy it is very easy to be too harsh on yourself and thereby further undermine your ability to think straight and/ or work out things constructively.

This is how low self-esteem starts taking root in your mind. This is when negative thoughts start building up in your mind telling you that you are not capable enough, wise enough, and prepared enough to handle the situation. Have you heard yourself saying things like:

- I am not good enough for this. I could never be able to do this. (Inadequacy)
- I am putting in so much effort. What if it's not enough? (Performance fears)
- I know I'm unlucky. No matter how much I work, something happens and everything will get ruined at the eleventh hour. (Victim syndrome; things beyond one's control)
- What if at the end of it, I am seen as an idiot and they'll laugh at me and my ideas? (Importance to external factors – others' opinions)

In most cases, this inner voice that pulls you down is wrong. But as long as you listen to it, you will not be able to trust yourself enough to do anything about it. It is then an easy slide into negative thinking and negative actions.

Stop negative thought as soon as you can. You need to believe you can, if you want to achieve anything good for yourself and others around you. You need to not only believe, but be convinced that you can.

I Can – Can I?

You would have heard about the adage, "If you think you can, you can; if you think you can't, you can't". This says it all. The moment you believe you can, you will be amazed at your strength to fight any situation given. The moment you make up your mind to fight it, your strength to do so would double. It does not matter that you would invariably face some minor or major setbacks; in the end you would indeed succeed.

The difference, the only difference between a successful person and a failure is that the successful person keeps going, no matter how many times he falls; the failure gives up and stops trying to get up. You lose when you stop trying; as long as you try, you will always find another way and another way – and at last, you will succeed. Thomas Edison failed 1001 times before he could invent the bulb. Was he upset? Not at all. He said he found 1001 ways of how not to do it. This is positive thinking at its best!

When you feel weak and helpless, it is more often than not, because your thoughts make you feel that way. What are you thinking? Your thoughts focus on the negative, i.e. on what could happen if you fail.

- "Oh God! What if my plan does not work?"

- "What if I don't do it right?"

- "What if people would find it ridiculous? What if they laugh at me?"

- "What if my work is misunderstood or rejected or found wanting?"

- "What if I lose everything I have?" – and the list goes on.

These are doubts; doubts that have the ability to change your "I can" conviction into "Can I" question. When doubts and negative thoughts take root in your mind, negative feelings are created, which lead to complete paralysis. Unless checked in time and eliminated systematically, negative thoughts and feelings would over time, kill your passion, will to move forward and ability to act.

To fight and counter negative feelings, you need to first recognize them as the trigger to your unhappiness. Imagine that you are your best friend and you are asked for advice.

This would help you look at these negative thoughts and feelings so much more objectively.

The Negative Feelings

Negative feelings never come alone. Along with the feelings of self-doubt come others that are as detrimental to your happiness. These negative feelings are the outcome or extension of low self-esteem, which result from excess negative thinking. There is a point when you want to logically justify what you are feeling and that justification turns into self-destructive thoughts.

Jealousy

You start blaming your inadequacy, worries, or perception of what feel/ think about you on others who are more successful than you. Anyone around you who is successful becomes the focus of your jealousy. Why him? Why not me?

As these thoughts start developing in your mind, you become more tied up by the negative picture of yourself, which you have projected in your mind, i.e. that of a helpless victim of circumstances.

Since you are jealous of others, you would not prefer to help them and hence, further diminish your ability to make friends, to be a team worker, to connect to others towards a win-win situation.

Fear

Your feeling of inadequacy would introduce fear into your mind and make you timid and complacent. You will be afraid to take any risks whether at work or in your personal life. You will be afraid to stand up to bullies, because you do not believe that you can win such a confrontation. You will be afraid to ask what you deserve and settle for whatever you get because you will be afraid you will be turned down and/or ridiculed if you ask for more.

Fear is one of the most debilitating of negative feelings. It clips your wings and mocks at you until you lose all interest in what you do in life – professionally and personally.

Anger

The feelings of inadequacy often lead to extreme frustration, which in turn will seek something or someone to blame. You do not like to believe that you are found wanting; instead you blame your parents, teachers, spouse, children, God, circumstances – anything and anyone other than you.

In your anger, you cannot see reason or logic and you would further destroy all possible chances for advancement in your work or professional life. Anger is one of the most destructive of all negative feelings.

Check out my book Anger Management for a more in depth analysis of this.

The Negative Talk

Where is this all coming from? Unhappiness, negative thinking, and negativity – all come from negative self-talking.

"But what is negative self-talking?" you ask. This is what you say to yourself when you commit a mistake – small or big. It is the little voice in your head. Imagine you have committed a blunder, what would you say to yourself? What would be the dialogue you would be having with yourself in your mind? Negative talking would go something like this:

- "God! I hate myself!! I am such a klutz!"

- "I can't do anything right. I am total idiot! Can't believe I am such an idiot!"

- "Of course, it would be a disaster! Can anything be okay if I do it? I am the king of imbeciles!"

- "I deserve such a kick in the @$# for this!! I am so totally useless!"

Does this sound familiar? Negative talking is when you give yourself a dressing down for any mistake you have committed – big or small. Even if and when you are forgiven by others – your boss, your spouse, and your friends – you continue to berate yourself mercilessly.

The Negative Action

Negative talk will gradually wear you down. Unless you fight it really hard, you will soon start believing that you are indeed worthless, hopeless, powerless, and useless. Just reading these words together make you feel small and depressed right? Now, when you feel undermined and unappreciated inside, you automatically assume that everyone else will see you the same way.

To protect yourself from getting hurt, you will act defensively and be closed about everything around you. Here is how the negative action starts.

Procrastination

Since you do not feel good about yourself, you tend to procrastinate. You simply do not want to start the work because:

- you feel that you are not good enough;

- you are scared that you would be criticized;

- you do not want to risk failure;

- you are too depressed to start; and so on.

Procrastination for whatever reason would interfere with your performance and bring about more and more negative thoughts and more negative action. This will set off a vicious circle that will only push you lower and lower.

You need to STOP procrastinating and take charge of your life today. Now. Take action NOW because you can, and because you are worthy of much better things.

Sometimes you need to just think; "Screw it, let's do it!" That is the mentally you need to engrain into your system. Don't think, just do it.

I also have a book outlining great ways to overcome Procrastination. It will really kick start your mindset to get up and seriously get things done.

Mind Clutter

Negative thoughts would have you worry about everything you do. Instead of thinking constructively and progressively, you crowd your mind with so many plans and end up totally overloading your mind. Imagine a room filled with clutter – can you work in such a room? Can you even think straight when you are surrounded by clutter and distractions?

Similarly, when the mind is filled of negative thoughts you stop thinking productively. Your mind will become your own enemy. You start doing something then leave it midway because you thought of something else that is important. By the end of the day, you would have gone through a thousand things – but have nothing completed.

The next day you do the same thing – and soon enough your mind is a whirlwind of activity – but whatever you do, nothing gets done.

Stop running helter-skelter and working without results. Take a few days off and draw up a plan. What you need to do, what you can do, where you need help, what is the time plan, what skills you need, what needs to be outsourced – and so on. Plan and go by your plan. Suddenly, all becomes clear and possible. Everything will fall into place and you realize something great – you CAN do it.

Giving Up On Dreams

Negative thinking pulls you down. It tells you, you cannot dream. Or if you can dream, you cannot make your dreams come true because you simply cannot. Many people believe that inner negative voice, shoot themselves down even before they even start and never even attempt to realize their dreams.

This is one of the worst outcomes of negative thinking. You stop enjoying your life. You start believing that life is a punishment to be endured and you have to do the best you can out of your circumstances – but without hoping to be happy.

Never give up on your dreams. Dreams are the color of your life. Fix your eyes on your goals, map your road and go for it. With the right planning and committed work – you CAN do anything you want to do; achieve anything you want to achieve.

Can't Say "No"

Negative thinking very often affects your self-esteem. When you suffer from low-esteem the last thing you want to do is create enemies – because who knows when you need an ally or someone to bail you out from a mess. You do not want anyone to think badly of you – so, you never say "no" even when it almost kills you to accommodate the request.

Pull yourself together and start respecting yourself. You need to be the No.1 in your own life. If you do not respect yourself, if you do not love yourself, if you do not take care of yourself – why should anyone else?

Next time when someone asks you something you do not want to do, say "no" politely and firmly. Practice a few times in front of the mirror so you're sure you can say it well when the time comes. After a couple of times, you will realize that it is not as difficult as you thought – and it does feel so wonderful to be free to do whatever you want instead of what others want you to do.

Chapter 2: Positive and Anti-Positive

Have you ever thought about how certain people stand straight in the face of the worst calamities and come out looking unscathed and how others seem to crumble at the first sign of trouble? How some people can stay positive come-what-may and others be so fragile in the face of trouble?

You will observe that people who are by nature positive, possess certain attributes that not only save them from wallowing in grief and self-pity, but also radiate positive feelings around them.

7 Positive Thinking Attributes

Let us look at a few of the most important attributes that would encourage and establish positive thinking. These are the attributes that you need to develop, sustain, and focus upon to maintain a positive attitude towards life and everything that comes your way.

Confidence

Ah! Confidence! Who does not want to have it? Who does not want to feel confident? *"Be confident!"* This is an advice that is so often heard but hard to act upon. You can recognize a confident person anywhere. He or she would stand out in a crowd. They are magnetic, inspire admiration and more often than not a little envy.

"How can they be so self-assured?", "Do they have any misgivings?", "Are they not afraid of failure?" "Are they too wise or too stupid?" - these are some questions that would play in your mind when you see a confident person. But let us come to the most important of all questions – Why is confidence important in positive thinking?

Confidence is very important because this is one very special attribute that measures your vision of self. Based on your level of confidence you would be labeled as a person with arrogance, confidence or low self-esteem. If you think you are too good at something, you become arrogant or over-confident; if you think you are just right you become confident; if you think you are not good enough, you develop low self-esteem.

This tells you one thing – you need to stay in the middle. Neither you should become too cocky, nor should you be too gun-shy. It is important to stay real because unless you have the right goal, you cannot reach the right destination. Confidence becomes harmful when it is in excess or is too less and has a negative effect instead of a positive one.

Confidence - Too Much or Too Little?

When people are over-confident, they tend to take many things for granted and that is the time they commit mistakes and land into trouble. Some people learn from the trouble and realize their level of competency; some people allow failure to break their spirit and lose themselves in low self-esteem. When people have low self-esteem on the other hand, they tend to underestimate themselves even when they succeed. Instead of acknowledging their abilities, they'd rather credit it to "luck", "circumstances", etc.

You cannot think positive or expect positive things when you have a distorted image of self. Each one of us is special. While it is true that no one is born perfect – and perhaps will never be perfect – it is also true that each one of us is special, unique and excellent at something. Sometimes, that "something" is not immediately obvious, but it does not mean that it is not there.

My youngest daughter once told me, "Dad, what will I do when I grow up? I am just not good at anything. I am not special." She was telling me this when she was in just 2 years away from high school. She was comparing herself to her elder sister (by just 5 years) who was an ace photographer and recognized her passion since she was about 7 years old.

I told her, "Baby, we'll cross the bridge when it comes. Let's not worry about what we do 2 years from now. Let us look at what we are doing now." I asked her, "What do you like to do now?" She thought for a while and answered miserably, "Nothing. I really have nothing in mind."

"This is because you are still thinking in terms of "what is acceptable". Forget about what-should-be", I said. "Think of what you want to do - period." She said simply, "Act and dance." I was a little surprised but nonetheless, I told her to go ahead and take part in as many plays and dance recitals there are in the school.

Two years after, my girl was chosen on full scholarship by the leading acting school in the country. On completing the acting degree, she went on and learned classical and modern dance forms. Today she acts in a half-a-dozen plays in theatres across the country, she dances professionally and models or a living. She makes a small fortune at the age of only just 23 and what is most important is that she is happy because she found herself. She loves what she is doing and she is doing what she loves.

Confidence – It Has To Be Just Right

Coming back to "confidence" – it is easy to see how the right amount of confidence can change your life. Had I pushed my girl into a profession I thought "safe", she would have gone my way, but perhaps would have always remained with the belief that she was "good at nothing". Had she gone ahead and signed up for acting in movies when the offers came in immediately after she completed school, she would have burnt out quickly due to over-confidence.

Either way, she would have lost real happiness. By staying level headed, ensuring that she is qualified and skilled for the profession that gives her most pleasure, she became a confident person who has nothing but success in her path.

The Dunning – Krueger Effect

Named after the scientists who studied how the level of confidence is influenced by self-evaluation, the Dunning-Krueger effect is when the higher skilled person feels inadequate because he see others floundering at the task he find too easy and effortless. In the same line of thought, the less skilled person thinks he is better than the rest because he is not looking at himself realistically; he feels he can do better, he is convinced that he is doing well and cannot accept that he is wrong.

Why Does It Matter That You Should Be Right?

Confidence matters because you need to believe in yourself. You can think positive and be positive only when it is in the right amount; only when you learn to make that self-evaluation realistic. In other words, you need to believe that you ARE special. Look at yourself as a critic and identify your strengths, weaknesses, threats and opportunities (SWOT).

Make a SWOT analysis of yourself and work out a realistic plan to improve. As you pass each milestone of your plan, you will find that your confidence grows, and with it your positive attitude about life in general and everything you do. Unless you believe in yourself and back yourself up all the way, nurturing a positive attitude may be quite difficult.

As a confident person you will enjoy many tangible benefits that would work to further boost your positive attitude.

1 - You are attractive romantically – studies show that people are more attracted (romantically) to confident people than to physically attractive people. Confidence becomes an irresistible trait both for men and women. Sometimes, just a direct unambiguous sign from a confident woman is enough to set in motion a date.

2 - You are more likely to succeed at climbing the ladder in your profession – as a confident person at work, you become more visible and you can get promoted faster. This becomes a good cycle for you, as the more you are appreciated, the more confident you are, the better you perform, and the more promotions you are likely to get. There are enough studies that show the correlation between confidence and success not only at work but even at school.

3 - Confidence has you putting out the right foot – as I explained earlier, "confidence" means "I believe I can". As long as you believe you can, you can. It is this belief that will drive you through life's setbacks as you'd see them as temporary obstacles. If you are overconfident or have low-esteem, obstacles can be devastating. Your insurance for success is ensuring that you truly "believe that you can".

How Do You Improve Confidence?

It is all well and good talking about how great confidence is and how it encourages positive thinking and positive attitude in your life. However, it is totally another thing to do something about it – if you are not exactly there. So, what can you do to get there? Fortunately, it is easier than it looks. Here are a few very simple things you can do to nurture the right degree of confidence in you:

1 - Introduce daily workout in your schedule – I cannot even start describing how important this is. Before you decide that this is not something you can do, let me tell you that "workout" does not and should not translate into "gym". You can simply walk and that would be enough of a workout. Physical activity will leave you full of feel-good endorphins and good energy. Besides, it would ensure a healthier body and mind, which will have you see the world through positive connotations.

2 - Dress the part – practice dressing to match your image of your successful self. It is extremely important that you behave and look the way you want to be. Experts often advice "fake it till you make it" and you'll have it sooner than you imagined. Invest in your wardrobe, grooming and accessories. Dress for success. People respond to what they see – and you respond to what people expect of you. Look the part – very soon the image of what you want to be and what you are will merge into ONE.

3 - Pay attention to your body language – if you are sad, angry, anxious or afraid your body language will portray that to others. Pay attention to your body language. Often, by choosing a confident posture your mind will respond positively. You will find the response to this reverse technique quite amazing. Learn what the body language that projects confidence is and practice it until it becomes your second nature. Positive thinking will be a direct outcome.

4 - Share knowledge freely and happily – be a teacher. Not as a profession, but in every aspect where you are a master. You'd be surprised how many things you know when you decide to share your knowledge. If you see anyone stuck, looking for help, potentially benefitting by something you can teach – DO IT.

Teaching others something you know best provides an amazing feeling of satisfaction that nurtures confidence. Whether you are great at computer programing or cooking – at what does not matter; what matters is that you are great at it. Enter competitions, talk about it, be there when someone needs advice – this not only builds you as expert in certain areas for others, but also in our own eyes. It is important that you BELIEVE you are special.

5 - Work at what you don't like about yourself – please note, I did not say what your weaknesses are, but what you do not like about yourself. Why is this important? It's important because what you do not like about yourself is the first thing that will drag you down into negativity. Simple things like "My nose is too big" "My accent is bad", "I feel like an idiot when people talk about politics".

Well, do something about it. Eliminate or at least reduce to minimum your mental irritants about yourself. Liking yourself is extremely important. You should be able to feel good about everything you project as your image – looks, intelligence, ability, etc. While it is true that you might not be able to completely eliminate all – you can always work towards improving on each of these negative points.

Just being aware that "this is something I am touchy about" is good progress. Then, doing something about it – whatever you can do, will further diminish the irritant. With it at the minimum, your confidence will blossom and so will your attitude towards everything in life.

6 - Be yourself – it makes sense, right? If you look closer at yourself however, you will be surprised at how many times you are actually trying to be someone else – who your parents want you to be, who your boss wants, who your spouse wants, etc. Sometimes, you are emulating others knowingly or unknowingly – your hero, one of your parents, someone you admire, etc.

Borrowing a few traits and mannerisms is no problem. It's actually good; however, when you start trying to be someone else it becomes harmful. For one, you are telling yourself that you - as you are – are not good enough; secondly by doing so, you will always be a duplicate instead of an original. Third and most importantly, is that your own nature will surface no matter how much you try to over impose something else on it – and when it happens, you will lose all the ground you gained by pretending being someone else.

Is it worth the trouble? Definitely not. Be yourself. Love yourself. Respect yourself. Forgive yourself. Improve yourself. Stay ORIGINAL. There is nobody as good as you at being YOU. The more you accept yourself as you are, the more positive and confident you will become.

7 - Become an expert – be an expert at something you love. Successful people find ways to do what they love for money. The adage, "Do what you love and you will never work a single day in your life" is so true. Ask yourself this – what would you do if you did not have to work for a living? What would give you most pleasure to do every day, day after day? What would have you galvanized and out of the bed feeling charged and happy every morning?

The answer to these questions represents what you need to do for a living. For one, you would become the best at it, simply because you love it; and secondly, you will enjoy it so much so that success would be a logical outcome to your efforts.

Now, let us say that your profession and what you genuinely love to do are at present two different things. Is this depressing? No need to be. Become an expert at what you love, even if that is not your profession/ career. You will find that gradually you will be recognized for your expertise in that field and more often than not, you will end up earning from it.

This is a more gradual way to move into your area of preference, but you will find yourself levitating towards those things where you are an expert. As your image grows in the eyes of the world and yours, your confidence grows and so would your overall positive attitude.

Love

People who are positive about life are people who love themselves and others. This is not romantic love, but love that makes you empathic towards other people, animals, plants, and to everything and everybody around you. Have you observed how when you learn about someone doing a kind thing it makes your heart go, "*aww*"? You feel good just knowing about it; that is the power of love.

Bring love in every aspect of your life.

Love yourself

The first thing you need to do is love yourself. Sounds simple. "Who doesn't?" you would ask. You will be surprised knowing that most people do not. Take this simple test and you will find out whether you love yourself enough, too much or too little.

Q1. When you look in the mirror, what do you do?

1. Berate yourself for something; there is always something that you've done wrong...
2. Smile a big one; say to yourself, "Looking goooood! Look out world, here I come!"
3. Say, "Oh God! I so hate the way I look. Nothing sits properly on me."
4. Observe all the things that you do not like about yourself, grimace and move away.

Q2. You receive a compliment. What do you do?

1. Beam happily and say "thank you". Pat yourself on the back for scoring.
2. Say "thank you" quickly and move away embarrassed.
3. Brush it off saying, "Oh, it's nothing. Anyone could have done a better job."
4. Become totally embarrassed by it and do not respond.

Q3. For a feeling of well-being what do you think you need?

1. Find yourself spiritually.
2. Live life king size. Work hard and play hard.
3. Money, money and more money.

4. Buy something. That's the only thing that makes you feel good.

Q4. In your priorities, "me-time" ranks as:

1. Somewhat important – you do "me-time" stuff only when you have the time.
2. Most important – you put the "me-time" as No.1 on your priority list.
3. Not important – what's all this about "me-time" – this is a total waste of time.
4. Least important – "me-time" is there, but expendable in case something else comes up.

Q5. You completed a major work. What do you afterwards?

1. Keep fretting about things that you've done wrong, berating yourself to no end for being stupid.
2. Worry yourself sick that something would be wrong somewhere.
3. Try to check it again to see whether you could find ways to improve upon it. There is always room for improvement. You want it perfect.
4. Celebrate big time, happy that you've done a great job.

Q6. Choose the statement that best describes you.

1. I need to study some more and get my next degree/ diploma.
2. I'm making loads of money working from my home.
3. I am on the lookout for a new game to play.
4. I want to earn a little extra doing anything at all.

Q7. I am a failure in my life. Do you agree?

1. True. I constantly berate myself for not living to my full potential.
2. False. I'd fail only when I stop picking myself up. Quitting is not my style.

Q8. What do you do when you feel low?

1. Take it seriously. You take out time and do all it takes to get back on the track.
2. Eat, eat and then eat more. Food is so comforting.
3. Bitch about life, your hard times, and everything to everyone whom you could catch.
4. Push it in the corner of the mind and ignore it and pretend all is well.

Q9. Which statement is closest to what you feel?

1. It's very difficult for me to change. I am what I am; take it or leave it.
2. I can always change what I want to change about myself. I have that much will power.
3. I wear plenty of hats; it is important to conform to social expectations to be successful and wanted.
4. I have so many people to blame for my present condition.

Q10. I am okay with my weaknesses and faults. True or False.

1. True. I forgive myself for my defects. Where I can, I work on overcoming my faults.
2. False. I cannot be flawed. I am perfect.

Q11. I can laugh at my mistakes. Actually, it's fun to be able to laugh at yourself. Do you agree?

1. OMG! Never. I would be mortified that I made a mistake. I would not sleep for days thinking about it.
2. Most often. Life is too short to take stuff seriously!
3. Sometimes, I find mistakes funny; it all depends how bad I screwed up.
4. No. Definitely not. I don't acknowledge mistakes; they make me look small.

Q12. I am not good enough. Do you agree to this statement?

1. True. Yes, I am never good enough.
2. False. I am happy with who I am. I definitely am good enough just the way I am.

Q13. Friends ask you out, when you find you are coming down with the flu. You are feeling quite sick. What do you do?

1. Go even if you feel sick like a dog because you don't want them to think you are a snob.
2. Excuse yourself because you'd rather go to bed and sleep it off.
3. Go just because you cannot say, "no" to them.
4. Decline the invitation because you do not feel you deserve having friends at all.

Q14. Nothing is lovable about me. True or False?

1. True. There is not one thing great about me.
2. False. I am totally lovable. There is so much in me that it worthy of love.

Q15. I am very comfortable by myself. True or False.

1. False. Without people around me, I feel alive. I need people around to make me feel happy.

2. True. I love my own company. Solitude becomes me.

Q16. If I were to disappear tomorrow from this world, not one person would miss me. True or False?

1. True. No one likes me. Don't blame them. I don't like myself either.
2. True. I am nothing and nobody. Totally part of the background. I wouldn't notice myself.
3. False. Of course, people would. I am significant in many people's life around me.

Q17. When you feel upset or stress what do you do?

1. Play games on my computer or mobile phone. Enough with the real world.
2. Meditate. Think. Reconnect with self and try to find ways to mend.
3. Nothing like a drink when you are down. It picks you up all the time.
4. Lose myself in the TV or a bestseller. Nothing like watching TV or reading a book to numb the pain and chase the blues away.

Q18. Among friends and at work place, I have set clear and non-negotiable boundaries.

1. False. I can never say, "No". I hate myself for it.
2. True. Yes, because I can say "No" – sometimes in words and sometimes in action.

Q19. You find someone criticizing you. What do you do?

1. It destroys me. I feel like it's the end of world for me.

2. I put my feelings on hold until I check whether the criticism is true or false. If found true, I work to improve in those areas. If false, I ignore it.
3. I totally tear that person apart. I will bring out the worst possible criticism about that person and shut him down.
4. I would wallow in self-pity and shame for a very long time. My recovery time from criticism is very slow.

Q20. You find you have committed a mistake. What do you do?

1. Pretend it never happened. If I accept it, everyone will brand me as a failure.
2. Berate myself into the ground for being so stupid.
3. Find ways to punish myself to erase the terrible guilt.
4. Forgive myself; will learn from it and try to avoid making such mistakes in the future.

Result of the quiz:

Give yourself **1 mark each** for the following answers; the rest mark with 0 (zero).

Q1 – 2, Q2 – 1, Q3 – 2, Q4 – 2, Q5 – 4, Q6 – 2, Q7- 2, Q8 – 1, Q9 – 2, Q10 – 1, Q11 – 3, Q12 - 2, Q13 – 2, Q14 – 2, Q15 – 2, Q16 – 3,Q17 – 2, Q18 – 2, Q19 – 2, Q20 – 4.

Total the score and see the answer:

Score 1-5

You need to love yourself more. You tend to put yourself last on every aspect. You do not feel happy about your life or about yourself. You feel you don't deserve anything good that comes your way and are terrified that whatever happiness you feel might go away if you enjoy it too much.

You need to work hard at recognizing that you are UNIQUE and SPECIAL. You deserve love and you are lovable. **This book is written for YOU**. Work hard to bring in positive thinking in your life. You need to play the leading role in your life. Right now, you are not even a character role...

Score 6-10

You realize that you need to love yourself more, but spend too much time focusing on what is not rather that what is. You are unable to assert yourself among friends and colleagues at work, for which you end up frustrated all the time.

You need to recognize that you need not be perfect in order to be loved and respected. Your family, friends and colleagues all appreciate you; they take advantage of you because you let them. They will still be your friends if you say "no" every once in a while and you will feel better about yourself. Put yourself on your priority list. Things will change for the better.

Score 11-15

You are aware of your plus and minus points and you are more or less okay with both. You tend to look at the glass half-empty too often and allow it to bring you down. You need to focus on the good things and build on it. Work on the flaws that can be corrected and learn to accept what you cannot change.

With a little effort, you can lead a rich and rewarding life. Learn to highlight the positive, nurture it and believe in it. Happiness and success – both will be yours.

Score 16-20

Perfect score. You know the importance of believing in yourself. You are a positive and confident person. You know what you want and go for it even when it clashes with the opinion of others. You know to make friends and keep them without compromising on your principles and goals. You are at home with who you are.

Stay positive. Work at staying there. There is a thin line between confident and over-confident. Be careful that that line is not crossed.

Loving yourself is one of the most important pre-requisites to mental and physical wellbeing. Thinking positive is a direct outcome of it. Without self-love, you will never give yourself enough of a chance to find happiness. Without self-love you will be lost in a world of negativity. You cannot let that happen, right? Here are a few simple ways to kindle that love within you; adopt as many as you can.

1. **Stop comparing** – you are UNIQUE in every way possible. There is ONLY ONE YOU in this whole world. Stop comparing yourself to others. Success and failure are just opinions of others. History is overflowing with instances where people were stamped as failures during their lifetime only to be declared geniuses after their death.

2. **Physical appearance is NOT as important as you think** – you could be thin, fat, short, tall, strikingly attractive or just plain to look at. The actual you is much more than your physical appearance. Close your eyes and think of the first 5 people you truly love. Now check each one of them carefully –

more often than not, you will find that these people are not exactly the best lookers on earth. However, in your mind's eye they are perfect; even beautiful. Why? Because their personalities make them beautiful. Stop worrying about how you look. You are perfect just the way you are.

3. **Exercise** – this is one thing that can work wonders for your mind, body and spirit. Besides the fact that it will keep you fit and healthy, exercising will make you happy, energetic and full of life. Many found that 30 minutes brisk walk actually improved their mood quickly and it stayed for the whole day.

4. **Find a thing where you are the best** – if you do not know it yet, find it. Look for it. It is there. Be relentless until you find what fires you and then pursue and perfect it. It's an amazing feeling to know that you know something better than anyone else. Write about it; talk about it; teach it to others, help others understand it better – be a MASTER.

5. **Spend time with people whom you love and love you back** – make time to spend with your loved ones – family and friends. Enjoy their presence, feel their love, love back.

6. **Have a "me-only time" at least once a month** – you need to take off at least once a month and do something that spoils you. Treat yourself to whatever you like. A fishing trip, camping with friends, a night out, shopping, a movie, special meal, whatever make you delightfully happy. Do it. Do it regularly. You're worth it.

7. **Read books** – reading is a wonderful habit. It sharpens the mind and expands imagination. It brings you in a world where only you can go; and you can go there as many times you want, whenever you want. Reading can expand your horizons like no other thing on earth.

8. **Spend time outdoors** – soak up the sun rays, allow rain to soak you to the skin, enjoy the outdoors as often as you can. It works wonders on your mind and body.

9. **Let go of the regrets** – everyone has done something yesterday they regret today. However, regrets, guilt, pain are emotional baggage that cause negative feelings. Let go of the past and live in the present. Try your best not to repeat past mistakes; make amends where possible and let go where nothing can be done.

10. **Stop hanging on dead relationships** – it is normal that people grow apart in some cases. This does not mean you are not lovable anymore or that you are flawed. Neither is the other person. It just means that you grew apart. Stop hanging on to dead relationships. Let go of people who don't love you back. Look for those who do and build on those relationships.

11. **Resolve issues as soon as possible** – you said something hurtful, you did something that hurt someone you love. Resolve it immediately. You were hurt by something a loved one said or done? Resolve

it immediately. Keeping feelings bottled up will only increase frustration and pain. Clear the air immediately – especially with loved ones.

12. **Take health supplements** – identify the best all-natural health supplements according to your age and health condition and take them regularly. A healthy body will promote a healthy mind. Crankiness, depression, mood swings are often the result of nutrients/ minerals/ vitamin deficiencies.

13. **Indulge yourself every once in a while** – how often is up to you. But do go and get yourself something that you would want very much, but do not actually need. Spoil yourself. Be your NUMBER ONE friend.

14. **Take care of your looks** – it's very important that you like how you look. When you are dressed in a manner you like (and know you look good in it) you promote an inner confidence that is irresistible to others around you. Take pains in getting to the point where you say "Wow" whenever you look in the mirror.

15. **Be selfish about your time** – whether at work or at home, be selfish about your time. Get the most out of it and do not allow others to encroach into it. When at home, keep the office away. Have clear cut off hours. When you are at office, ensure that your work has the priority it deserves. You will achieve more and be more relaxed; and contrary to common belief, it is not very difficult to do it.

16. **Build a favorite movie/ books library** – we all have movies and books that we love. Build a library where you keep all those movies and books that you love the most. Watch/ read as often as you can. Sometimes, just looking at your favorite book or movie DVD is enough to make you happy.

17. **Have at least ONE hobby** - hobbies are our play time. Ensure you have at least one hobby that delights you. Ideally, you should work carefully into monetizing your hobby so one day you would earn a living with your hobby. Loving your work is one of the best recipes for success and happiness.

18. **Travel** - if you don't like travelling, try learning about other places, cultures, foods, and customs from the internet or TV. If you like travelling, do travel as much as you can. It's wonderful seeing new places, new people and learning new things.

19. **Laugh often** – make it a point to look for the lighter side of everything. Believe me, most things have a lighter side. Laugh with all your heart and do it often. It improves your health, mood and relationships.

20. **Dance with abandon** – play loud music at home and alone – if you are shy to do it with friends – and dance with wild abandon. There is something about dancing with closed eyes, to the rhythm of your favorite music that cannot be compared with anything.

21. **Do something good with no expectations** – it's a wonderful feeling when you do something good for

someone who cannot return your kindness. Do it as often as you can.

22. **Be non-judgmental** – this is a hard one, but worth its weight in gold. Give everyone the benefit of the doubt. Do not judge anyone by their past; everyone can commit mistakes and then change for the better. That includes you, as well. Every day is a potential for a great tomorrow.

23. **Do stuff for others** – do thoughtful things for others. Cook a special meal, buy a small gift, take a photograph, get a pet, give a hug – anything that you think would bring a smile on your loved ones face. Makes you feel like a million dollars!

24. **Eat healthy** – no need of becoming a health freak, but it is important to watch what you eat. You would not put water in your car, instead of gas and expect it run, right? Your body is a very sophisticated machine; if you give it half a chance, it would not only maintain itself, but also repair itself when necessary. Moderation is the key.

25. **You are Number 1** – you cannot please everyone, so stop trying to. No matter how much you try you will always have someone grumbling about it. Just do what your heart says is right and good. It's only you that you have to please. Do a great job there and all will fall into place.

Enthusiasm

Enthusiasm is defined as "intense eagerness and enjoyment". People who are positive see opportunities in everything around them. It's like every day is a gift to be unwrapped – there is mystery, surprise, happiness – all good emotions. It is true that you may not always feel the same level of enthusiasm about the things you do.

Sometimes, you may get a project that you are not too hot about, or an assignment that is more headache than pleasure or a client that drives up the wall. However, staying positive is the only out of any sticky situation. Why?

Because when you stay positive your mind looks for solutions and you will be amazed to realize that whenever you look for a solution you will find it. Conversely, when you are negative you look for something to blame it on, indulge in self-pity and then you resign to your "fate". The difference is clear. A positive person will think constructively and find a way out – and there is always a way out if you are willing to look for it.

There is this story about a man who had suddenly come into an inheritance of 10 acres of land in Florida or Arizona. Happy that he was about to get rid of his debts he relocated to the new place with great hopes and expectations. He was thoroughly disappointed to find that the whole 10 acres were desert land – only sand. His hopes to have a farm were dashed to the ground. To add to his immense misery he found that the area was filled with rattlesnakes, which are deadly poisonous.

For a while he was overwhelmed by the turn of events. He came with expectations that these 10 acres would help him make a good living for his family. Instead he found only desolation, unworkable land and inheritance taxes to pay. In addition, he had exposed his family to the deadly danger of being bitten by rattlesnakes.

After a while he snapped out of the self-pity mode, ignored the what-he-could-not-do thoughts and looked around at what he could do. The first thing he felt he needed to do is make sure that his family consisting of wife and two sons aged 5 and 7 were not bitten by the snakes.

He made an enclosure and learnt how to keep the rattlesnakes at bay. He bought anti-venom and taught his wife how to use it. He taught the children to stay off outdoors unless he or their mom was with them. He learnt how to catch the snakes without getting bitten with and without implements.

Then, while he was getting rid of some of the snakes around the farm he came upon an idea. "When life gives you lemons, think of making lemonade" he thought. Why not sell the skin of the snakes and perhaps even the venom. Happy with the idea he researched and within a week he had a few good orders on his hand.

In less than a month he had set a cottage industry that could process some 500 snakes per day. Life was looking up again. Of course, it was not the way he envisaged it, but fortune was smiling on him. It did look like this desert farm - which at first looked useless – would fend for his family.

One day, when he was delivering the snake skins, one of the truck drivers asked for some snake meat. He gave it to him and asked the truck driver what he needed it for. "I am going to eat it" the truck driver said. "It is very tasty and my family loves it."

This set the ball rolling on another tangent for our hero. He realized the potential of selling the meat along with the skins, but he needed to solve the problem of preserving the meat long enough. The solution was canning. He immediately set up a mini canning center and now he was earning more from the meat than the skins.

In less than 5 years, this man who thought he hit the rock bottom when he relocated on the rattlesnake farm - as he called it – was now rich beyond his dreams and what is most important, happy. He was happy because he could make the best out of what he had and came up a winner.

Moral of the Story:

Never let your enthusiasm die out. The solution might not always be the way you saw it; and just because it did not work out the way you wanted, it does not mean that success is no longer possible.

Faith

Faith is belief in something that you cannot see, feel or hear. Faith is a very important attribute to positive thinking. Often used in connection with religion, having faith does not mean you have to believe in God. It rather means than you believe in your ability to succeed, in the ability of the Universe to respond to your prayers and fulfill your wishes.

The adage, "Faith moves mountains" is all too familiar – and true. The human mind is the most powerful force in the Universe. It connects the mortal body with the soul and Universe (or God/ Providence/ Cosmos). Faith fixates it on unwavering belief – and it is that belief that makes impossible things possible.

History is full of people who have achieved the impossible because they had faith in their own abilities to conquer and conquered.

Adaptability

Adaptability is one other trait that will ensure a positive outcome. Let us say you are planning for a picnic and it starts raining. Instead of getting all upset and angry that your picnic is lost, you could change it to a marathon movie-watching day or indoor games tournament and so on.

In life there is perhaps only one thing that will always remain constant; change. You will find change at every step, in every aspect and when you are least prepared for it. You have two choices – adapt or perish. The ability of adapting to change is what will make you successful and give you happiness.

Develop Your Ability to Adapt

Charles Darwin said, "It is not the strongest of the species that survives... It is the one that is most adaptable to change". It is extremely important that you develop an attitude of adaptability. The better you adapt to change, the better you would fare in life. Here a few tips to help you hone your adaptability skills:

1. **Keep Calm** - this is the first thing you need to have in the face of change, especially sudden change. If you have a tendency to panic or lose your cool, learn techniques to control it. Simple methods such as

counting to 10, taking a walk (remove yourself from the stressful area) or drinking a glass of cold water.

2. **Take Every Change As A Challenge To Learn A New Thing** – it is always beautiful to learn something new. Every change brings along with it plenty of new things to learn. Look at every change as an opportunity to learn something new. Learning something is a positive experience; with time you will enjoy every change because you get to know new things.

3. **Improvise** – learn to improvise. Do not get stuck on anything. If you do not have the right part, person, or circumstance – improvise. There is always a way. Sometimes, the new way is actually better than the old one. Like the person who found himself owning 10 acres of desert land rampant with rattlesnakes – make the best of what you have.

4. **See The Larger Picture** – most of the time we tend to focus on details and lose the larger picture in the process. Small details will more often than not create a false sense of disaster, while when put in the right perspective, they would be almost insignificant. Learn to distance yourself from the details and see the big picture whenever you feel overwhelmed. Ask yourself – would this still matter to you say in a year, 5 or 10 years from now?

5. **Get Help** – some people feel that if they ask for help or assistance it reflects bad on them. On the contrary, it only shows that you are smart enough to understand that you cannot know it all. Whenever

you feel you do not know or cannot do something look for expert help. Be ready to learn. Be quick to accept that you do not know something. As long as you seek knowledge, you will not have the time to indulge in negativity.

Helpful

Have you observed how kind people are almost always smiling? People who empathize with others and are helpful feel peaceful inside. "Helpful" does not mean only lending a hand to those who are in need. It has a much larger connotation. It means giving the benefit of the doubt when someone wrongs you, it means sharing knowledge with your colleagues and it means sacrificing a little comfort to adjust someone's needs, and so on.

Generally speaking, being helpful means "do onto others as you would like others do onto you". It might be quite trying sometimes, but being helpful will give you immense happiness and earn you a horde of goodwill and well-wishers.

Being helpful will keep your heart full of love, will help you forgive, will have you see the brighter side – in other words, it will keep you positive.

Attitude

Nothing is more important than your attitude when it comes to finding happiness and success. A positive attitude will take you to great heights while a negative attitude would destroy you. If you look closely, the outcome of everything you do depends upon your attitude.

4 Tips to Ensure a Positive Attitude

A positive attitude is your most powerful tool against trying times. Here are 5 foolproof tips to develop a positive attitude and maintain it that way.

1. **Look For The Silver Lining** – everything happens for a good cause. Sometimes, the "good" is not easily visible. You need to believe that everything that happens, happens for good. Learn to look for the silver lining. In the gravest situations, such as when you lose a loved one there would be a purpose to it. You cannot say "good" in the face of such tremendous loss, but such deep pain often gives us the ability to be more empathetic, loving, forgiving and helpful to others.

2. **Think Out Of The Box** – just because it is done "this way" earlier, it does not mean it has to carry on like that forever. When you are faced with a problem, be quick to think out of the box. With every obstacle you overcome you will become more adept at seeking and finding solutions to seemingly impossible situations.

3. **Be Incurably Optimistic** – expect a good outcome. Do not be the one that carries premonitions of disaster. Negativity breeds negativity just as positivity breeds positivity. Be the solution seeker and finder; refuse to be bowed down by negative thought and fear of failure.

4. **Move On** – positive people do not dwell on setbacks however grave they are. They move on. There was a story about an Indian king whose son fell gravely ill. He announced a huge reward for anyone who could cure the child. The best doctors in the kingdom attended to the prince and the king rarely moved away from his bedside.

This went on for 5 months. The king was beside himself with grief and pain watching his son die every day. He invoked the gods, paid special homages, and tried every possible cure – nothing changed. The prince died. The next day, the king attended the tasks of his kingdom, which had suffered because he could not give any time.

Everyone wondered how the king is able to function when the prince had just died. His chief minister gathered courage and asked the king, "Your Majesty, isn't it a little too early for you to attend to work? Would you rather not rest a little and allow the grief to subside?" The King replied, "As long as there was something I can do, I will do. Now, my son is no longer alive. There is no sense in grieving about something than cannot be helped. I'd rather use my time productively."

When Positive Thinking Is NOT Good

You may be surprised to learn that positive thinking might not always be good. So, what can be wrong with something positive and how can things go wrong? We've all heard about too much good is bad. This is the case with positive thinking as well. Let us take a look at situations when positive thinking is not exactly a good thing.

Ignoring The Negative Side – positive thinking does NOT mean that you ignore the negative aspect of any situation. Rather, it is important that you pay objective attention to it. "Objective" is important, because the sooner you become emotional about it, you will lose your ability to take clear decisions. Hence, do not in the name of positive thinking ignore the dangers of the negative side.

For example, let us say your company is downsizing because it is suffering loses. Nobody is at fault; a dip in the economy has caused it. Now, if you think that positive thinking would protect your job, that's wishful thinking. Instead, as a positive person, you would look and take cognizance of the danger of losing your job and take steps to minimize the trouble if that happens. You could inquire about other opportunities, look for part time jobs or other means of earning, cut down expenses to the minimum until the storm blows over, etc.

In this way, you would be prepared if the axe falls and you would not have too much too worry. You'd suffer a setback, but you would be able to handle it. Closing your eyes to the danger and hoping it will not happen is positive thinking misplaced.

Ignoring A Hopeless Situation – in some situations, such as a bad relationship, a bad job, a bad investment you need to say "enough". In such situations, positive thinking would have you hope for amelioration, which actually would hurt you more than help.

Positive thinking should help you to realize and accept situations that have generated negative feelings. If you feel unhappy constantly, if you find that your identity suffers, if you feel that you are not making progress in spite of your best efforts, cut off from that situation.

Be like the sunflower – follow the sun. Trust your instincts; what are you feeling? Are you happy? Are you comfortable with who you are, what you are doing, how you are living? If the answer is no, it is time to stop doing it.

Expecting Results Without Effort – positive thinking is like nutrition to the mind and soul. Positive thinking is not magic. Assuming that positive thinking would attract money, happiness, good job, promotion, love – is just fanciful thinking. You need to work for it; you need to be optimistic about it – but not wishful. Without action there is no fruit.

When positive thinking promotes inaction and wishful expectations, it becomes poison and unless controlled, it would destroy you.

Expecting Smooth Sailing - positive thinking does not mean that everything you do will turn out right or smooth. Assuming this would leave open to pain and disappointment. Expect obstacles, failures, betrayals, pain as part of life. Positive thinking does not protect you from these; it gives you strength to overcome them. You need to understand the difference and stay positive, especially in the face of trouble.

Expecting All Your Wishes Come True – people following the Law of Attraction believe that the Universe listens to them and provides whatever they ask. This is 100 percent true. At the same time, assuming that all that you wish for is good for you is fanciful thinking. Yes, your wishes would come true as long as they fall into line with your karma and your purpose of life.

Allow for a few things to be illogical and unexpected. Assuming that positive thinking will provide you with all that you want, will bring you disappointment. Your wishes will come true as long as they are aligned with the "big picture". There are times, when you cannot see the "big picture"; you need to allow for it and trust and believe things will work out in your favor.

Chapter 3: Can Positive Thinking Help You?

Can positive thinking help you? Of course it can! It has been proven so many times, in so many ways. People succeeding in spite of all odds, people doing feats that were conceived impossible, people recovering from impossible illnesses and injuries – and so many others.

You might be aware that "pet therapy" is today a scientifically accepted therapy that brings people back from depression and revives the will to live in geriatric people and terminally ill patients. Introducing an animal in the lives of people who suffer from depression/ terminal illness triggers feelings of love; this in turn activates positive thinking, which in turn pulls people out of depression. Isn't that amazing? This is the power of positive thinking.

Why?

Positive thinking has the power to make you healthier, more active, more successful and of course, most importantly happier. Therefore, positive thinking is something you need to introduce and sustain throughout your life.

Research shows that positive thinking improves the immune system, accelerates healing, improves memory, enhances your working capacity and even slows down aging. Besides, positive thinking keeps your mind open to new possibilities, which often results in discovering new paths and new options in your life.

How?

Positive thinking thrives where the mind is at rest. Hence, to ensure that you encourage positive thinking and sustain it, try one, more or all these steps:

1. **Meditation** – this calms your nerves and eliminates the harm done to your mind and body by stress. People who meditate regularly are known to be able to learn faster, work harder, avoid health problems, and be more empathic to others. You don't need to go through a complete how-to course on meditation to benefit from it. Just 10-15 minutes of the basic tenets will do just as well.

2. **Writing** – writing about positive experiences helps the mind relax and focus on the bright side. Research studies found that people who have written about positive things for just a week have experienced better moods, improved ability to focus, better memory and improved health. Science accepts that writing good things attracts positive thinking, which in turn is beneficial to both your mind and body.

3. **Play** - stay in touch with your inner child. You need to allow yourself to laugh and see the lighter side of things every now and then. Children fall, cry and then bounce back laughing like nothing happened. Adults need to do that more often. Playing, laughing, doing silly things improves your emotions and draws in positive thoughts.

Make time every day for fun and play. This will help keep your inner child alive and the easier you find to laugh at a difficult situation the more positive your thinking will become.

4. **Socialize** – it is not for nothing that it is said, "Man is a social animal". Socializing helps relax the mind through

sharing of experiences, empathizing, sharing joys and sorrows and overall connecting with another human being. Connecting to another person normally uplifts the mind.

5. **Happiness first** - don't put success before happiness. Many people put conditions on their happiness such as, "Once I become the CEO, I will be happy" or "If I lose just 10 pounds, I will be okay." Don't. Do not put conditions on your happiness because once you start doing it, you never stop. Hence, you need to enjoy your life today –unconditionally. Tomorrow is never yours; what you have is today.

6. **Smile a lot** – try this in the mirror. Frown as hard as you can and smile. You will observe that, try as much as you want, you cannot frown and smile at the same time; and when you smile you cannot be angry. Smiling is like a therapy to the mind. When you smile, you say to yourself, "I'm okay", "I'm good", "All is well", and "I'm happy". It helps relieve tension and lightens the mood. A smile is like an "urgent call to positive thinking". A smile is also infectious! Try this next time on a complete stranger, whether they be a passer-by, the assistant at your grocery store, the bus driver on your journey home, just look them in the eye and genuinely smile. You will notice that whatever mood they may be in, they will reciprocate with a smile back to you. Share the happiness!

When?

Positive thinking will come to your help especially when you are going through a difficult phase. Positive thinking will benefit you in every situation, but it will be especially good in difficult phases such as:

- when you are depressed, positive thinking will motivate you to look beyond the gloom;

- when you are sick, positive thinking will boost your immune system and accelerate healing;

- when you are faced with challenges, positive thinking will get your mind to look at new solutions and opportunities;

- when you want to make new friends, positive thinking will make you more attractive and help you identify the good in others;

- when you face self-doubt and low self-esteem, positive thinking will renew belief in yourself and build your confidence;

- when you go through any grief, positive thinking will find you a way to climb out and find ways to cope.

Chapter 4: Attracting the Power of Positive Thinking

A number of research studies have affirmed that positive thinking is hugely beneficial. Here are a few methods that have proven that positive thinking works – and it works so well.

The Law of Attraction

The Law of Attraction or LoA as it is commonly referred to, is a well-known concept that states that your life is what you make it. Literally. If you think negatively, you attract negative forces into your life and thereby invite difficulties in every aspect of your life. On the other hand, positive thoughts would attract positive experiences.

At the root of this concept is the belief that the Universe is a continuum of the mind and responds to the thoughts and actions you put forward. Hence, when you think in positive terms you meet positive results and when you think in negative terms you attract negative results.

According to Law of Attraction, all you need to do is believe in absolute terms that what you want will happen. There is no space for any negativity. This is why in the affirmation statements the first and only rule is that there should be no negation; in other words, the statements should be coined using only positive terms. This is because according to the LoA when you use negative words – even if it is for a positive statement – it will attract the negative.

For example:

- Correct statement – I will be courageous.

- Incorrect statement – I will not be afraid.

Positive Affirmations

Positive affirmation is another very popular concept. This involves writing down a few key positive statements (affirmative) repeating them again and again until your subconscious mind internalizes them completely. It is not necessary that at the time of writing them down, these affirmations are true. Some examples of positive affirmations are:

- I am confident.

- I am good at what I do.

- I love my life.

- I can do whatever I want, whenever I want.

- I am free.

- I am happy.

It is not necessary that you believe this when you say, or that these are true. Nonetheless, you need to keep repeating it until – in time – you will believe it and your life will change for the better in the manner you visualized.

The Power of Prayer

Prayer is one of the most powerful of all tools for positive thinking. There are many reasons why people pray, but one of the most common reasons is that it provides inner peace. When you pray, you imagine God – this omnipotent, omnipresent and all-knowing being – in front of whom you need not pretend, lie or keep anything back.

You are completely transparent and the ability of opening your heart to someone without any conditions or the need to hold back anything is exhilarating and liberating. The prayer is highly therapeutic on many occasions such as:

- in times of grief;

- when you feel circumstances are totally out of your control;

- when you are afraid of the future, past or present;

- when you want something, but do not know how to go about it; and so many other ways.

Prayer calms the nerves, steadies the mind and opens it to new ideas and solutions that you might have otherwise not thought about. Prayer helps you to let go of the need to control your life, of the guilt of whatever you did in the past and of the helplessness of some no-win situations that you come across in life.

Prayer allows you to share your innermost fears, hopes, mistakes and insecurities without the fear of being judged or alienated. God is able to not only forgive all the wrongs you do, but also provide you guidance and open new opportunities and new directions for you.

Prayer helps you reset the score to zero and start again. It allows you to empty your mind and heart of emotional clutter and guilt baggage and start again. Prayer clears the path to positive thinking and gives you a chance to start again.

Happiness: A Definition

According to the dictionary, happiness is a state of contentment, satisfaction, carefreeness, joy, pleasure, wellbeing and so on. Happiness is a feeling that puts you on the top of the world. Generally speaking happiness is a positive feeling – but if you want to go into particularities, you will find that happiness has a separate connotation to every person. Hence, the term is difficult to define in absolute terms.

What is important to know is that "happiness" more than success is the main goal of every human being – whether they know it or not. People who put their success before happiness are actually chasing happiness – because that is what they feel when they achieve their goal.

However, there is one important thing that is often ignored about happiness, which makes the quest difficult and sometimes totally impossible.

Some people tend to search for happiness outside, when they should in fact look for it from the inside.

Keep this one very important fundamental truth in your mind at all times, if you want to find happiness and hold on to it, i.e. happiness comes from within you and cannot be influenced by any external factor. The moment you start searching or validating it through external factors, it will escape like sand through a tightly closed fist.

Positive thinking is one of the most powerful paths that lead to happiness. It makes you realize that you have the power to control your feelings even when you cannot control the circumstances that you come across every day. It also tells you that you can choose to be happy or to be morose about anything in your life. When one makes you happy and the other miserable it is not difficult to decide which the best choice is.

Vibration: Keep It Above 500 MHz

Did you know that the Earth vibrates at 528 MHz? The human body as everything else you can see possesses a certain amount of energy; each object and living thing vibrates with energy. While inanimate things cannot be influenced by vibration, human beings can.

Each emotion, each thought has a vibration. The positive emotions vibrate above 500 MHz, while negative emotions vibrate below 500. To enjoy positive energy in your life, you need to ensure that you maintain your vibration at 500 MHz or above.

There are two ways to ensure that you get your vibration to 500 MHz and keep it there and above. The first is to identify what brings it down and avoid it; the second is to identify what bring it up and practice it as much as possible.

Factors That Lower Your Vibration

There are many factors that suck your positive energy away. Check out the list below and try eliminating or at best, reducing these factors as much as possible.

1. **Negative energy people** – we all know these types. They grumble about everything, they are constantly whining and complaining, they are the perpetual victims. They could be your family members, friends, colleagues, neighbors, etc.

   While it might not be possible to eliminate such people from your life, you can distance yourself a little and or teach them to raise their vibration by helping them focus on positive side of life, getting them to meditate, exercise and so on.

2. **Watching and/ or partaking violent activities** – watching games that involve fights, violence, etc. or taking part in such activities. Choose something that gives your mind peace instead. Watching violent movies, horror shows, and anything that generates fear and anger within you brings your vibration down.

3. **EMF or Electro-Magnetic Frequencies** - that emanate from all the devices that we consider indispensable today such as TV, mobile phones, computers, etc. interfere with your vibration negatively. Minimize their use and where possible eliminate them.

4. **Stress** – stress is a killer. Science has proved this beyond any doubt. You perhaps did not know however, that stress brings down your frequency by inducing negative thoughts and feelings. Eliminate stress from your life through meditation, exercise, reading, playing music, etc.

5. **Negative emotions** – anger, fear, hatred, holding grudges, guilt, regrets, jealousy, revengeful thoughts and violence are negative emotions that bring down your vibration significantly. The lower the vibration, the worse the negative thoughts – thus, it creates a vicious circle that will destroy your peace and happiness. Snap out of it by focusing on building your ability to focus on positive things and positive energy.

6. **Bad diet** – your body is a super-machine; it can do some extremely amazing things. However, its capacity to function at its highest level is dependent upon what

you feed it. The type of energy it generates is directly relevant to your choice of diet. Eat junk and you bring your body's pH levels down and trigger negative energy and lower vibrations.

7. **Toxins and pollution** – exposure of your body and mind to toxins and pollution pulls down the level of vibration within your body. Drinking alcohol, smoking, substance abuse, exposure to pollution, etc. interferes with your level of vibration.

   Toxins are not only in physical terms; your mind also could be affected by toxic thoughts. Gossiping, conspiring against others, cheating, stealing, hurting others, etc. are toxic to the mind and have the same effect.

Factors That Increase Your Vibration

Just as there are factors that bring your vibration level down, there are factors that boost it.

1. **Practice love and compassion** – try your best to be kind to every living thing. It is harder than you would think. Human beings somehow find it easier to be hurtful, believe the worst and do the worst; many in the name of "the greater good". A few examples of atrocities perpetuated by human beings – which are accepted as "normal" in many civilized countries and communities - are tests on animals, hunting for fun, bull fighting (and other animal fights), female circumcision, abortion of the female child, etc.

2. **Eat healthy** – focus on vegetables and fruit and remove yourself or at best minimize from processed foods and refined foods.

3. **Meditate** – contrary to common belief learning to meditate is extremely easy as it is beneficial. You need not meditate for hours on end; just 15-30 minutes per day would help you immensely. There are enough guides available online for free that would teach simple methods to meditate. Learn and practice daily, introduce it to your daily routine.

4. **Introduce yoga into your life** – yoga postures are designed to keep the body, mind and soul in their ideal state. According to the Vedas (ancient Hindu science manuscripts) there is nothing that yoga cannot cure. Learn and practice yoga daily; 10-15 minutes is enough. **Warning**: You need to learn yoga from a teacher/ guru. Never start with videos or any other self-teaching aides.

5. **Sleep well** – ensure that you have at least 6 hours of proper sleep at night. It is important that you sleep at night – 8 hours' sleep during the day would still fall short of 3-4 hours deep sleep during night. Sleep at the same time every day and wake up at the same each morning. Try not to eat anything at least 3 hours before you sleep.

6. **Laugh a lot** – read funny books, watch comedy movies, spend time with people who make you laugh, take yourself lightly as often as you can and laugh at yourself. Laughter has the ability to bring up your vibration exponentially.

7. **Cleanse your aura regularly** – there are many ways to do this. Among the simplest methods are:

   a. **Bathe in warm salt water** while visualizing that your aura is cleansed of impurities and harmful elements. Use unprocessed salts that have no chemicals such as Himalayan salt or sea salt. Table salt is not suitable for this process.

      Draw a bath where you add 2-3 handfuls of this salt. You could also use a few drops of essential oil of your preference. Soak in the water for about 15-30 minutes, while you visualize all the impurities being washed away.

      When it is over, rinse with a warm water shower. The salt bath should not be repeated more than once a week. You could also swim in the sea as its natural salty water has the same effect.

   b. **Smudging** – this is done with the help of a bunch of dried white sage. You can buy a smudge stick online. You need to light the stick up and allow the flame to go off. As it starts smoking, wave the stick from head to toe and all around you visualizing that the smoke purifies your aura and removing all that is harmful. Do this for a few minutes and then extinguish the stick totally by burying it in the soil.

8. **Adopt a pet** – animals with their unconditional love have the ability to raise your vibration. Adopt a pet and be responsible for its wellbeing. Their love will uplift you in many ways than one.

9. **Spend time outdoors amongst nature** – In Japan they have a wonderful tradition named as "Forest Bath". This is when one takes a break from the city life and walks through a forest allowing the sights, sounds and smells to wash away the man-made counterparts.

10. **Use essential oils** – smells like emotions, have their own vibration levels and have the ability to raise or lower it. Take the advice of an expert when you want to use essential oils for this purpose.

Chapter 5: The Tools You Need

In order to draw in the power of positive thinking in your life, you would do good to use some tools. Here are a few methods that will cement positive thinking as an everyday habit for you, which in turn will help you fulfill your life's goals and dream and find happiness.

Thoughts: What Are You Thinking?

We have seen earlier how important it is what we think. When you "talk" to yourself in your mind following a failure or any mishap, you are drawing a picture of yourself in your mind. That image imprints in your mind and stays there a very long time. If that picture is negative, everything you do afterwards will be negative.

It is important therefore to be careful about what thoughts you allow to dwell in your mind. You need to focus on the positive aspects of any given situation; and in those situations where you find it very hard to find anything positive at all, make an effort not to end up blaming yourself.

People with low self-esteem tend to blame themselves for everything that goes wrong around them; even those things where they had nothing to do with it. For example, they would say, "This happened because I am so unlucky." Or "This happened because wherever I go I bring disaster."

Focus on the positive aspect of any situation. Also teach yourself to catch those negative thoughts right in the formative period. You may not be able to help thinking, "Boy! I messed up big time!" but you can stop this thought from developing into, "I am so utterly hopeless and good-for-nothing!"

Learn to be quick in forgiving yourself and moving forward. If you have difficulty in doing that, just imagine yourself as a friend. How would you have reacted if that friend committed the mistake/ faux pas/ problem you did? It is often very easy to forgive a friends mistakes and also easy to convince the friend to "forget all about it".

Apply the same rules to yourself. Let go of the guilt and blame; learn the lesson and move on. Encourage positive thought through your mind and believe in yourself. Be your own best friend.

Attitude: Challenge Your Thoughts

You need a positive attitude to sustain positive thoughts long enough to benefit from their power. If you have a defeatist attitude, you will end up defeated. You need to focus on developing a positive attitude and sustain it. You need to believe in yourself, be confident that you can face any type of situation and find solutions to any problem that comes your way.

Changing your attitude is easy as long as you keep a close watch on your thoughts and do not let them get away into the negativity. You can change your attitude in 3 quick steps:

1. **Find what you need to change** – it is very important that you first identify which traits are holding you down. The exercise you did earlier to identify who you really are would come in handy now. Identify one (or more) negative traits that influence your attitude and target it for change. Attempt to make one change at a time.

2. **Find a role model to make it easier to visualize** – to make things easier, identify a role model whom you would

like to emulate. This would make it easier for you to visualize the changes you want to see in yourself.

3. **Visualize the result of the change** – see in your mind's eye how this change in attitude can change your life. What does change mean to you? Success? Better understanding among friends? A loving relationship with your spouse or children? – and so on. Project that image as vividly as you can because the clearer the image, the easier it will be for you to transition to that change.

Belief: Boost the Strength of Your Mind

Nothing works without belief. You have to believe it can happen before you see it happen. You also have to develop a set of beliefs that support a positive attitude and promote positive thinking. Run through the following beliefs and work them into your life steadily yet firmly to ensure that you stay positive even when things don't look so good at first sight.

1. **It does not matter what people say about me** – the moment you pay attention to what other say about you, you give them control over you. Do not bother about who says and what they say. They are entitled to their opinion; also how many people can you please, even if you tried? Best is to keep doing what you feel is right and ignore anything and anyone who thinks otherwise.

2. **I have the freedom to be me** – you should not need to put on a façade in front of your friends, loved ones, work mates, etc. You need to be yourself – the original person, nothing else. The moment you imitate anyone, you are saying loud and clear, "I am not comfortable with being myself".

3. **Life really sucks sometimes, but I can do a lot of good out of what I have** – this is important because life indeed will kick plenty of dirt in your face. Instead of sitting there and crying in pain, the best way is to take cover and think of how to overcome it. Never ask, "Why me?" because bad things do also happen to good people, it's just that they handle it in a different way. Hence, it may happen to you, too. At that time, pray that you have it in you to see the brighter side and move ahead.

4. **I'm down today and that is okay** – there will be times when things do not go the way you planned. Life is not always a bed of roses; sometimes you get more thorns than flowers. At such times, you need to keep in mind that "these things happen" and will pass.

5. **I'm grateful for all I have** – very often when we encounter obstacles in our lives we focus on the "have not's" instead of being grateful for what we have. It is extremely important that every day, you count the blessings you have one by one. This is especially important when you are going through a hardship because it will deflect your pain and put things in a better perspective.

6. **I made a mistake. It's ok. I'm learning**. Don't kill yourself over the mistakes you do. Use the lesson and move on. Every wrong turn leads somewhere – perhaps not always the best way, but nevertheless a new way and there is something to learn from every mistake.

7. **Things change; it's ok**. Only change is permanent. Expect everything to change. Nothing lasts forever – good or bad, things will change. Sometimes, things take a turn for the better and sometimes for worse. You need to be prepared

for change and face it head on. The more you run away from change or resist it, the harder it will be for you to be happy.

8. **My happiness comes from within**. Your happiness does not depend upon ANYTHING external. It is there within you. It is the way you love and respect yourself. It is the way you allow anything external to affect you. It is NOT coming from money, love, friends, acceptance, and professional success. It comes from within. It comes from believing that you are special, that you deserve the best and will get the best. Nobody should be allowed to control your happiness; that is your prerogative.

9. **I choose to stay around people who appreciate me**. Make it a point to surround yourself with people who appreciate you for what you are. Remove yourself from people who put you down, who make you feel bad about yourself, who limit your dreams, who weigh you down. Get away from any negative influence because it will drain your positivity about life. You are the company you keep.

10. **If I'm asking whether it's worth it, it is not**. Listen to your gut feelings; especially in matters of love. If you find yourself asking, "Is this worth it?" it is NOT; because when it is, you will know 100% that it is. There is no scope of doubt when you are in that special relationship. You totally know. When the question comes up, it is because there are things that need you to compromise. Don't. Don't compromise on anything that gives you happiness. Laugh at your mistakes, allow yourself to break rules, live your life in full – you have only today; you never know what tomorrow brings.

11. **I am making a difference**. Do something good for someone. Make a difference in somebody's life. Be the answer of someone's prayers. It is hugely liberating and

joyous to know that you are able to make a difference – for the better – in someone's life. Make it a point to do at least ONE good deed every day, big or small. You will find that your life feels blessed.

12. **I have no expectations and I am never disappointed**. This is perhaps the most important rule of life. No matter what you do – at work, in your personal relationships, clandestine help – NEVER expect anything. The moment you expect anything, you are open for disappointment because more often than not, you will not get what you expect. The best way is to never expect anything; hence, anything that does come to you becomes a bonus to be celebrated. Unfulfilled expectations can make you bitter and resentful – and rob you of your happiness. Don't allow that to happen.

Will Power: This, I'll Change

You have the will power to change what you do not like. Many times we compromise with life because we are too tired to struggle anymore. Don't. Do not stop until you get what you want out of your life. You owe yourself that much.

This little story will help you understand better. There was this person – Jeremy - who was kind, hardworking and helpful. He got a lousy job, which was paying much less than he deserved and worked him into the ground. It was difficult for him to leave because he had a family to support and the market was not too good for looking for another job.

Eric and Mark were Jeremy's closest friends. One day Mark was out of the way angry about Jeremy being stuck in a bad paying job and all. Eric replied, "You get what you deserve. Don't worry about that." Mark was shocked. He knew that

Eric loved Jeremy; they were childhood friends. So, how could he make such a remark?

Eric explained, "See, life hands you ups and downs. Sometimes, you just have to stay down for a while. But if you are good, and you know what you want and what you are worth, you will not rest until you get what you deserve." In other words, until you think you got all that you are worth you will keep struggling to get more. You stop only when you think it is enough.

The knowledge that you deserve better than you have today will give you the strength and will power to fight your way through to reach your goal. Hence, you should never feel too bad because you are stuck in bad relationship, bad job, bad choice of career – make the best of what you have and move forward towards your goal.

The lesson here is that you need to be truthful to yourself about what you want out of your life and what you actually deserve. Do not compromise on your happiness. Have the will power to change and keep changing until you get what you deserve – and more.

Next time you find yourself stuck in any type of situation that you do not like, say to yourself firmly, "This, I will change."

Self-Motivation – The Force That Takes You Forward

Motivation is the driving force that gets you to do anything that you need to be done. To do your best, you need to keep your motivation high and focused. For example, you find work because the need for money to live well motivates you. You marry because the need to start a family motivates you.

Without motivation, you would not have a reason to get out of the bed in the morning; it is that important.

Self-motivation is always a challenge and something that needs to be worked upon constantly. Contrary to common belief, it is not too difficult to keep the levels of self-motivation at the highest levels. Here are a few hacks that will help get there and stay there.

Motivation Hack #1: Shout It From The Rooftops

You are planning a new goal that is killing you? Push yourself into action by letting everyone know you are doing it. Post on Facebook, share it with your family, friends, and colleagues; you will instantly have built the stage for self-accountability in front of so many others. Not likely that you will fail to achieve your goal, now.

Motivation Hack #2: Join an Online Forum/ Group

This helps as you would be able to share your joys and challenges with people who have walked on the same path. There will be advice, encouragement, failure stories, success stories and overall enough to keep you motivated to keep going.

Motivation Hack #3: See It and Believe It

Take a picture/poster showing you with the goal already achieved and place on your desk/ fridge/ wall/ computer – where you can see it all the time. Nothing can motivate you better than the joy you feel seeing it done.

Motivation Hack #4: Have a I-Can-Do-It Plan in Place

Motivation works best when the goal seems achievable. I will be a millionaire by 30 will not push you too far when you are 18. But if the goal is broken into I-Can-Do-It bites, such as need earn X-amount of dollars per week, save X-amount per month, invest X-amount of dollars per year, and so on – suddenly it all becomes possible and workable. You believe it; you go for it.

Motivation Hack #5: Partner in Crime

Get someone (or more people) do the same thing as you. This will not only give you peer pressure, but also add a little more excitement to achieving your goal since you now have competition; a challenge of who does it better and best.

Motivation Hack #6: Just One Step At A Time

Sometimes the task at hand is killing you and you'd give anything to get rid of it, to sweep it under the carpet, to never start it at all. At such time, just get yourself to move one step at a time; just ONE step is enough. You have to run in the morning? Just one step at a time: put on your running shoes. Once your shoes are on, you'll automatically move towards the door, close it behind you and start running.

Motivation Hack #7: Change It To A Fun/ Pleasure Thing

Think creatively and you will find ways to make even the worst possible task into a pleasure you look forward to. For example, let us say you have this horrible project you have to complete. Set your everyday goal to end with the most delicious fresh berry tart, or a favorite cup of hot chocolate. Add something to it that will make you look forward to complete it and voila! You have the satisfaction of getting the task done and the little pleasure that you built into it to make the going sweeter.

Motivation Hack #8: Break The Big One Into Many Small Bits

I need to lose 48 pounds. Sounds like an insurmountable task. I need to lose 48 pounds in 2 years. It sounds much better now, right? I need to lose 1 pound every month. Now that is something that can be done and will make you happy that you can. Breaking a big tough task into small achievable ones will keep you going smoothly.

Motivation Hack #9: Celebrate Every Milestone Crossed

Break every goal into mini-goals and then celebrate it with self-reward every time you achieve one. This will boost your confidence and make you look forward to the next goal.

Motivation Hack #10: Allow Yourself A Slip Up

Believe it or not, not allowing yourself a little leeway actually can kill your plan to achieve your goal. It's okay to slip up a little every now and then. However, build in proper checks and balances to ensure you stay on track. For example, make it a rule that you cannot let yourself skip/slip two days in a row; and once you slip, you cannot have another until a week has passed. In this way, you can let yourself go sometimes, without killing your project.

Motivation Hack #11: Keep a Track of the Ground You've Covered

It is immensely motivating to see how far you've come. Let us say, your goal is to lose 50 pounds in 2 years and at the end of 6 months you have lost 10 pounds, you look at it and can't stop saying, "Wow! I can do it!" Tracking your progress is an exceptionally powerful way to keep you motivated.

Motivation Hack #12: Educate Yourself On The Topic of Your Goal

Read about our goal, about people who have achieved your goal, about the ways to achieve your goal, about hacks to achieve your goal easier and so on. In other words, study all the information you can on the subject. Knowledge is power; and power is very motivating.

Motivation Hack #13: Get A Guru

Have someone who has been there guide you. This could be a professional coach, your boss, your colleague, anyone who has walked the path you are walking on right now. It's wonderful to have someone with whom you can discuss face-to-face, the ups and downs you are experiencing about achieving your goal.

Motivation Hack #14: Make It A Routine Or Adventure Time

Sometimes, it works to have a routine. Say, I will complete XYZ every morning before lunch break; or I will run 5 miles before 8 AM every morning. For some people this works fine, for others a routine becomes stifling after some time. What about adding a new angle – such as work from home on some days or in coffee shop; run on the treadmill in the local gym, or change the exercise for an equivalent one and do it at home. A change of scenery can change your mindset.

Motivation Hack #15: Help Others Do It

You cannot ever go wrong with this one. When you assume the mantle of a "guru" you can no longer allow yourself the luxury of failure. You've become an example and by definition you have to be the best.

Health: I've Got the Power

If you have everything and you have no health – you have nothing. It is very important that you maintain good health. Contrary to common belief, "healthy" does not mean boring, sacrificing or a strict discipline type of life. "Healthy" means learning to enjoy everything in moderation. Work, food, sex – all the pleasures of life, everything is good for you as long as it is done in moderation.

Your body is an exquisite machine that knows how to self-repair and maintain itself. However, in order for it to be self-sufficient you need to keep all its systems working optimally; and this happens when you eat right, work right, enjoy right, relax right and rest right.

Eat right – a balanced meal is very important. Make it a point to have as many vegetables and fresh fruit in your day to day menu. Meat is not bad, unless it is the main part of your meal, for every meal. Here are a few tips that will help you stay healthy:

- Avoid as much as possible processed foods and lean towards fresh and unpreserved food.

- Eat in smaller 4-6 meals a day, rather than 3 large meals.

- Always have breakfast. This is the most important meal of the day.

- Drink plenty of water. Dehydration is the root cause for majority of diseases.

- Take health supplements according to your age requirements. Multivitamins never hurt anyone; especially when you are not able to have a balanced meal every day. For women over 30, calcium is a good supplement, and so on. Don't go overboard with the supplements; but it is good to know what your body might need to work optimally.

- Go through detoxification process every 8-12 months. It is good for your body and mind.

- Choose home-cooked meals rather than eating outside.

- Go slow on the coffee and any other stimulants. About 2-3 cups a day is good – but anything more than that will dehydrate you and interfere with your sleep.

- Binge if you must on anything you like; but make it rare and in between. Let this be a treat for you – not a habit.

Work right – working hard is good. It helps you build your career/ business, generate wealth and feel good about yourself. However, you need to know that there are rules here that need to be followed if you want to enjoy the best of it.

- You know the saying, "Only work and no play, makes Jack a dull boy". Work hard. It is important that you give your all to your work. However, keep in mind that work and play need to be balanced to perfection for best results.

- Have more or less fixed hours for work and when you are off it, you are off it. Learn to compartmentalize work and personal life so both do not mix with one another.

- Family (personal) time should be as important as work time. No interference, no interruptions when you are with your family (or by yourself).

- Love your work and you will never work a day in your life. Look for ways to monetize your passion – and you will be delighted to work every day. It does not matter if the job you are doing today is not exactly your dream job – look for ways to get there and never stop until you reach your goal.

Enjoy right – having fun, partying, vacationing is a must-have for both mind and body. However, it is important that it is done in moderation and good taste.

- Partying until the early hours of the morning is great – if done once in a while; not every day of every weekend.

- Smoking is killing you. Quit now. If you are smoking for pleasure or out of habit make the effort to quit. You are poisoning yourself and those around you who are inhaling your smoke. Quit. Today.

- Say no to drugs. It always starts as "fun" and often ends in total tragedy. You can party without entertainment drugs. Firmly say "no" to drugs. This is one experience you need not have.

- Alcohol is fine when consumed socially. However, if you find yourself wanting to take more than 2-4 glasses every day – you have a problem. Do something about it. Now.

- Don't drink and drive. You risk your life, that of those whom you love and other people on the road. It is not seriously worth it.

Relax right – your body and mind needs relaxation. Ensure that you take out time for exercising, which is not only relaxing for your body but also your mind. You need not sign up for expensive and time-consuming gym workouts. Just go for a long walk about 30-60 minutes every day.

- Exercise every day. Choose a time that suits you best and do it every day – even on weekends and holidays.

- Learn meditation and practice it after work to ensure that you relieve the stress that has built up during the day. Stress is deadly for both body and mind.

- Follow your heart and pick a hobby that gives you pleasure. Every person has a passion. Find yours and lose yourself in that pleasure over the weekend. This will relax your mind and recharge it for the work time.

Rest right – resting is very important. It allows your body and mind to repair itself and do the overall maintenance wherever necessary. You need anything between 5-8 hours of sleep every day. Most doctors say that an adult requires 6 hours of night sleep, but some people feel okay with 4. Sleeping is as important – if not more – as eating right and exercising right. Lack of sleep can kill quicker than lack of food and water.

- Go to sleep at the same time every night; wake up at the same time every morning. This is very important.

- The night-sleep is what counts; you can sleep 12 hours during day time, but that will not help you as much as 4 hours during the night as it is during this time your body produces hormones which help at repairing and maintaining your mind and body.

- Eat your day's last meal at least 4 hours before you go to bed. Digestion slows down when you sleep and if you have a meal too close to bed time you will suffer from indigestion and other stomach-related conditions.

- Make up for lost sleep if you have to work nights for any reason. Your body will wear out quicker if it does not have enough quality rest.

- Lack of sleep or bad sleep affects memory, ability to focus and concentrate, ability to solve problems, and so on.

Physical Fitness: It's Possible Without Sweating It Out

Don't let the belief that exercising is tough to incorporate into you daily routine stop you from staying fit. You can exercise whenever you want, wherever you want. Check out these 20 tips and incorporate as many as you like into your daily routine. This will make exercising fun and the results will delight you as you would be melting calories effortlessly.

The Morning Hours

1. First-thing-in-the-morning exercise – you can burn 10 calories right at the time when you rise from the bed. Sit up straight on the bed upon waking, with your legs straight and lean slowly forward towards your toes until you feel the muscles in your back pulling. Repeat 3-4 times immediately after you wake up. Ensure you are slow and gentle with the stretches as your muscles will be pretty stiff first thing in the morning. Ease into it.

2. Balancing is an excellent exercise – when you brush your teeth stand and balance your body on each leg for 30 seconds each time. This would work out your core muscles and stimulate your brain. In addition, you lose about 40 + calories.

3. Drink your coffee standing up – Hold the table or any other available similar support, and lift one leg straight in front of you. Hold it there for about 3-4 seconds and then in one movement bring it sideways. Again, hold for 3-4 seconds. Repeat the process stretching your leg behind you. This is a great way to tone your thighs, quadriceps and hip flexors.

The Nine To Five Time

4. Use the stuck-in-the-traffic-time – you are driving during the peak hours. You would be bound to run into some terrible traffic jams. Use every time you step on the brake due to traffic jam as a means to tone your derriere and lose some excess calories. You need to squeeze the buttock muscles for about 10 seconds and repeat as many times as you can. This could help burn minimum 50 calories – even on an easy traffic day.

5. 'Pretend to sit' exercise – reading about this exercise would make you laugh; but you will find that this can help you burn about 70 calories just like that. As you go to sit at your desk – stop a few inches short from sitting and straighten up. You can do this even in the loo – if you can hold it. Aim at doing this exercise about 15-20 times every day, each time for 3-4 times holding the stance for about 3-4 seconds.

6. Phone time is walking time – use a wireless phone and every time you get a call, walk around your office or home. You could walk a few miles just with the talking on the phone. This would help you lose about 50 calories.

7. Move about – whether it is around your home or in the office try to do things in person. Walk around instead of asking others to run your errands for you. The to-n-fro walking would help you burn some serious calories, while interacting with people would improve your work ambiance and relationships. At home also, you tend to communicate better when you are active physically.

8. Wall push-ups – adaptation is the best gift humans have. You might not have the time to go to the gym, but you could just stretch your hand to support your body in a reclining position, leaning forward against any wall in your office and grab a few quick and highly effective, though unusual, push-ups.

9. Chair exercises – as you are sitting and taking care of your work, all you have to do is put your knees together and lift them as much as possible towards your chest. Do these exercise for 3-4 sets of eight; it strengthens the abdominals.

10. Weight is good – yes, you are reading correctly. Weight is good when you carry it in your hands. This would build your resistance and improve your mood. On days when you do not shop, make it a point to carry something that weighs about two pounds at least. An hour of carrying such a weight would give you the opportunity to lose about 30 calories.

11. Exercising at the pump: when you fill in gas, use one hand to support yourself on your car and stand on the balls of our feet and come down to your normal position. Do these ups-and-downs until the vehicle is fueled. You might get to do about 30-50 rises which would consume about 25 calories per session.

12. Window shop for weight control – this would bring a smile to any woman's face. The 'shop until you drop'

can be modified to 'shop until weight drops'. Here, you do not need to buy anything; just move around and try out as many outfits as you can lay your hands upon and watch the calories burn. Could get rid of about 60-80 calories.

13. Health in queue – whenever you are waiting in queue for anything, clasp your hands behind the back of your neck and squeeze the shoulder blades as tightly as you can. This not only refreshes you but also stimulates the nervous system.

The "At Home Time"

14. Put junk mail to good use - everybody receives junk, which is so annoying. However you could use it for positive things. Make a pact that for every junk mail or email you receive you walk a certain distance – say 500 yards or go up and down the stairs at home two times or similar goals. In this manner, you would have plenty of exercise every day – which is good for the regulation of your weight, keeps your mood pepped up, and stimulates your brain.

15. Use the stairs – the stairs for you can have many more uses than just getting you to the next floor up. When you are about to climb any type of stairs, try this: put your leg on the first step, bend it at the knee and shift your body from one leg to another. Do this for about 10 times and then alternate legs. It burns about 50 calories.

16. Dining table exercise – after dinner, when you would wait for dessert, you could do the following exercises. Extend your foot under the table and bend it at the knee. Squeeze a little and hold for about five seconds.

Repeat for 4-5 times and shift to the other leg. It helps sculpting your quadriceps and burns about 20 calories.

17. Relax and lose weight – you could be sitting in front of the television set sometimes. At such times, do some simple exercises that will relax and refresh you instantly. Keep your feet uncrossed. Hold the wrist of one hand and lift your hands above your head as if you were stretching. Feel the spine elongate. Hold there up for about 10-20 seconds and repeat holding the other wrist. Burns about 20 calories and make you feel as new.

18. Use ad time to your advantage – you would remember, if you ever read Archie comics that Jughead would run to fix a snack whenever a commercial came up. You could use the time to lose some weight. Do abdominal crunches until your favorite program comes back. You would be happy to know that in this manner you could count to 100 crunches and about be 30 calories short.

19. On the bed – before you drift off to sleep try this – lie on your back bend your knees and lift your hips; do it for about 10 times and lose about 20 calories, just as you turn in to sleep. You would definitely have some very pleasant dreams.

Weekend Bonanza Time

20. Singing - are you fond of singing? Try singing in a choir or just at home for about 20-30 minutes. A simple singing session like that would burn about 80 calories. Doesn't this make you sing for joy?

Chapter 6: Exercises That Help Positive Thinking

Positive thinking is a good habit and like any good habit it takes time to inculcate. Here are a few simple and very effective exercises and methods that will help you to think positive – no matter what.

Getting Rid of Worrying

What is worrying? Worrying is misplaced imagination. The problem with worrying is that it has the power to stress you to no end – for no actual reason because in majority of cases nothing happens. When you worry, you think about the possibilities of things going wrong.

You need to get rid of worrying. To do so, instead of worrying prepare for the worst possible scenario. Think beforehand, "What could go wrong here?" and prepare for any of those eventualities. Worry comes when you are not prepared well enough because it makes you feel helpless to the outcome.

Counter the helpless feeling by preparing for all possible mishaps that could be controlled. The rest you leave to the eventualities of life, what will be will be. Accept that you cannot control everything no matter what you do. So, give your best possible shot and leave the rest to fate.

Side by side, ensure that you have enough to occupy your mind when you think you are prone for a worry attack. If you have something to do, it is least likely that you will worry too much. Do something pleasant and happy – preferably for someone else.

No Complaints for 24 Hours

Have a "24-hours of no complaints" period as often as you can in your schedule. You could have it once a month or once a week. When this period is declared, the rule would be that you cannot complain about anything you find annoying, no matter what. Instead, try looking beyond it and do something constructive.

A nice story can give you a fair idea of how useful this method can be. A lady was shopping at a super market and observed that the cashier was very grumpy. She was snappy bordering on rude. The people she served responded with equal or more irritation.

When this lady's turn came, the cashier almost threw her change on the counter. However, the lady did not take offence; instead she smiled at the cashier and asked her full of empathy, "You had a rough day dear, didn't you?" Then, paying her a tip she said, "Here dear have a wonderful cup of coffee on me. It will make you feel better."

Surprisingly, the cashier smiled, accepted the tip and said, "Thank you so much. My daughter is in the hospital and I could not get off today. I am very upset. Thank you for understanding."

Very often giving the benefit of doubt is all it takes to make the day better for you and others. Unfortunately, we tend to jump to the worst conclusions when we should rather be a little empathic. Next time, when you feel like snapping a biting retort to someone rude, take a deep breath, count to 10 and reply with kindness. It will definitely make your day because you refused to allow the incident to make you angry; and it may change that person's day for the better, too.

3-6 Hours of Pure Kindness

Another way to make you feel good and encourage positive thinking, is to give yourself a 3-6 hours' time out when you should be kind to everyone around you. Be warned that this could be stressful initially, because you cannot get angry with anyone or say an unkind word, or do anything unkind to anyone – no matter what.

But with time and practice, you will learn to enjoy doing this. Empathy is one of the greatest gifts of mankind. Dalai Lama XIV once said, *"If you want others to be happy, practice compassion. If you want to be happy, practice compassion."*

The greatest gift you can give yourself and others is compassion. When you impose these hours of pure kindness, you will learn to see the good in every person. It is impossible to get angry with anyone if and when you see the good in them.

Like the example in the "cashier lady" story, you need to understand that when someone behaves badly it is because that person is unhappy for some reason. This person needs your compassion the most. If you practice kindness in spite of the response, you will realize that this helps you more than the recipient.

Kindness – when offered unconditionally - has the power to calm your mind and fill you with a tranquility that is beyond compare.

Thank You, I Appreciate It Very Much

Learn to appreciate others. Say "thank you" as often as you can; say it with genuineness and feeling. Everybody loves to be appreciated for what they do. It is wonderfully rewarding and motivating to receive a well said "thank you". Whenever somebody does you a good turn, no matter how small be quick to say, "thank you".

Learning to appreciate others will make it easier to appreciate the good things in your life. Every person has a long list of blessings, happy hours, good times – but we tend to focus on the negative – what we do not have, what we lost, what we would have had and lose the chance to enjoy what we DO have.

Whether you say, "thank you" to God, your friend, your spouse, your children, a stranger or anyone who did something for you, the benefit of it comes to you first. When you say "thank you" you realize that you received something nice and you have a reason to be happy.

Learnt to be grateful for what you have and say it aloud as often as you can. Say "thank you" as often as you can. It will make you happy.

Sorry, I Hurt You – Please Forgive Me

Just as it is important to say, "thank you", it is important to say "sorry" as often as it is required and with genuine feelings. Whenever you realize you have hurt anyone, be quick to express your remorse. Say "sorry" as soon as you can. This will clear the air and allow healing on both sides.

An apology put forth appropriately will always create positive energy. Try this experiment. Next time when you are in an angry altercation with anyone, take a deep breath and say, "I am sorry if what I did (or said) hurt you". See what happens. In most cases, when you say you're sorry the anger dissipates like smoke.

With the anger gone, good vibes come right back in and you will be surprised how good it feels for you as well.

It's Okay, I Forgive You

It is important that you can forgive those who hurt you as well. Often we carry a grudge forever, without realizing that the anger and hurt erodes the soul and mind. Revenge is a poison that you carry inside you. When you hold anything against a person who has hurt you, you are tying yourself to that person and reliving the hurt again and again.

Forgiving means letting the bitterness go, which in turn sets you free. All religions advocate forgiveness – with a good reason. When you forgive, you become emotionally free of pain. Try it; you will feel a weight lifted off your shoulders, literally. It is a wonderful feeling to let go of the hurt. Forgiveness is a gift you offer yourself more than the others.

Chapter 7: Be Positive - Your Plan of Action

By now, if you are following what is advised in this book you would've been able to get rid of most of your negativity, if not all. As a plan of action that will guide and keep you on the track, take a look at these steps.

Make the Effort to Look For the Good in Everything

From now onwards, every time you look at somebody or something make it a point to say something good first before you say or do anything else. Make the effort of identifying something good in everything you look at. With practice, you will find it easier and easier to do so.

Also, try your best to keep all that is negative unsaid as much as possible. Practice this – give your comments only when you have something nice to say (it should be genuine); keep all negative thoughts and observation to yourself.

Learn Meditation

In today's world, where stress is in every aspect of our lives, meditation is lifesaving. Learn the simple stuff, if you are not interested in understanding the complexity of meditation learn the basics of it and practice it every day.

For best results meditate every day at the same time. However, if you cannot have it put on a permanent schedule, meditate whenever you have the time. Do it every day though.

You Need To Learn To Say 'No'

When you do not feel confident about yourself you are always afraid of "what others will say". The opinion of others becomes so important that you cannot say "no" to anyone for anything. You feel obligated to accommodate every request that comes your way because you simply do not want them to "think poorly about you".

STOP. You need to learn to say "no" when you do not what to comply with a request for any reason whatsoever. You also need not give a reason for saying "no". As you get in tune with yourself and learn to value your own feelings above those of others, you will find the courage to say "no" whenever needed.

The transition will not be easy; and hence, you should be well prepared for it. When you say it, be polite and kind yet firm. There are three simple ways to say, "No":

1. **Say it straight and quick** – I cannot do it; I'm very sorry. Use a pleasant yet firm tone, and smile to take the edge off for both of you. Do not let yourself be pushed into a "yes", or you will not be taken seriously later on when you want to say "no" again.

2. **Say that it is "under consideration"** – the best way to say "no" without saying it immediately, is saying that you will consider it. "Under consideration" is one of the easiest ways to say "no". Saying "I'll get back to you on this" will buy you a little time to compose yourself for saying "no". Do not delay too much, though.

3. **An exchange offer** – when you cannot or do not want to do what is asked, you can dodge the

commitment by offering something lesser in exchange. Say, "I cannot do this. I am sorry. But what about if I can do this (XYZ suggestion) instead. Hope this will help you." In this manner you do not say an outright "no"; neither will you have to do what you are asked.

Keep a Close Watch on Your Thoughts

You need to practice catching your negative thoughts and stopping them right at the time of formation. Replace them with positive thoughts. Whenever you find destructive thoughts, berating thoughts, worrying thoughts running through your mind push them out with positive thinking.

Choose To Be Happy

When you are stuck in a bad situation or anything bad happens to you, choose to be happy. You are not a victim of circumstance; do not allow yourself to feel like a victim. Look for ways, find the will, take action and move towards your desired goal keeping in mind that whatever bad things you are facing today will soon pass away.

You Are Not Perfect – Live With That

Don't chase perfection because that guarantees you only one thing – frustration and unhappiness. It's okay to make mistakes. Be as forgiving to yourself as would be with other people's mistakes.

Aim for perfection in everything you do; that's good. It helps you challenge yourself to do better and more. However, do not let this goal blind you to the fact nobody's perfect. It's okay to have flaws; make the best of what you have.

Smile

Smile a lot. This seemingly insignificant act can fill your life with happiness. Smiling does not allow you to stay angry or upset. It also makes others around you feel good. Smile at anyone – known or unknown – in most cases it will attract another smile. A smiling face makes you feel good inside and it makes the recipient feel good as well.

Try to smile as often as you can. It will keep you relaxed and happy and make everyone around you happy as well.

Sing and Dance

Music, like smiling, does not require any language or time. Music has the ability to relax your mind and body as it has the ability to kill stress. If you don't like singing yourself, play some songs you like. Do it as often as you can. Some people find it calming to have music playing in the background at work. If that works for you – by all means do that.

Dancing too, has a very liberating effect. Whenever you can, turn the volume up and dance with abandon. It is amazing how good you feel after you do this. Dancing is an exceptionally good exercise as well.

List Your Blessings – Every Day

Every day make it a point to identify 5 things for which you are grateful. List these five things in writing and thank God or the Providence for these blessings. Gratefulness keeps your mind into the positive and will help you maintain balance when something does not go your way.

Help Someone

You have the ability to change someone's life. Do a good deed for someone. Be someone's wish come true. Make it a habit to identify someone who requires help – and you help them. Remember that help needs to be done with extreme finesse ensuring that the person who received the help does not feel looked down upon.

The help has to be done with utmost grace without hurting the dignity of the recipient or being condescending.

Conclusion

I hope this book was able to help you to fill your life with positive vibes and energy. With positive thinking you will find your life packed with limitless possibilities. Happiness is there waiting for you to receive it, cherish it and share it. Focus on the positive every time and on every aspect of your life and you will find that blessings come pouring in from all quarters.

Practice positive thinking every day and you will be assured of a rich and rewarding life. Positive thinking is like a magic wand which attracts only good towards you. It is not difficult and it costs nothing. Start today. Promise yourself that you will be happy and you'll take all the necessary steps to stay so.

Make your plan of action and start today.

Here is to your happiness! Stay blessed! Stay happy!

Finally, if you have enjoyed reading this book or found any form of value in it, then I'd like to ask for a favor, would you be kind enough to share your thoughts and leave a review for this book on Amazon?

I aim to reach out to my readers by providing the best value and quality content I can. Your positive review will help me achieve that! It would be greatly appreciated!

You can leave a review for this book by simply typing the following link into your web browser:

http://amzn.to/1LqTKM0

Thank you and good luck!

Hanif Raah

Preview of 'Time Management: The 24.5 hour Day'

Chapter 1: What Is Time Management?

"Time management" is by definition, the ability of organizing your time so you could optimize the benefits you get out of it. Paradoxically, the busiest you are, the less you get done. Hence, to be able to do more and better, you need to be the master of your time and not vice versa.

You see people today in a perpetual race to get somewhere, yet all they get is stress, heartache and health problems. You have people die of heart attack at 55 or even 45 because of stress – and stress is the result of lack of time management. You definitely do not want that.

Successful people, real achievers, the people whom you admire will tell you that working is very important in life; but more important than working hard is working smart. By "working smart" it means that you get more for the effort you put in, than vice-versa. Most people just work hard – which is a good thing, too. But if you want the BEST, you need to learn to work smart. You get that with time management.

Time management is the process that gives you mastery over your time. It sets you free to do what you want and when you want.

7 Reasons Why Time Management Is Good For You

Good time management will help you in every aspect of your life, i.e. at work, in relationships, with children, and for yourself. Here are the top 10 reasons why time management is a skill that you should master as early as possible.

Less Stress

Time management would ensure that you have total clarity about what you are doing and when you are doing it. It's like removing all clutter from your mind so you can see only what you need functionally. Hence, you will have minimum stress and maximum output.

Increased Output

Productivity increases by leaps and bounds since your mind is free from stress and hence, free to focus on the tasks that need to be completed without distractions. You not only complete the tasks you have set out to do, but also find time to do other things that until now you could not do because of lack of time.

Increased Energy

Recall how you feel when you complete a task that required your intense intervention. The satisfaction that you enjoy at the end of a work well done and completed on time releases the endorphins that make you feel good about yourself and more energetic. You will be ready to take on the next task.

Freedom to Do What You Want

With time management you will find enough time to complete your "work" and still have enough left to bond with your family on daily basis, socialize with friends and colleagues, take up a hobby, read a book – and in general do things that you would have otherwise thought impossible for lack of time.

Reduced Effort

You will find that with time management the effort you require seems less because your mind is calm and focused and you can concentrate your full attention on your work schedule.

Minimum Wasted Time

An unorganized person spends a lot of time searching things, redoing things, handling situations resulting from mistakes, and so on. With time management, you learn to work in a focused manner and hence, commit fewer mistakes (ordinarily resulting from stress from mismanagement of time). This also helps eliminating the time you would otherwise waste when re-engaging in a task you interrupted.

Increased Opportunities

Clarity of mind helps you think more creatively and hence, find more opportunities to grow. An uncluttered mind is more likely to open to new ideas that a mind burdened with 1001 things on it.

10 Mistakes That Can Kill Time Management

Before you even start looking for room for improvement, you need to identify and recognize the top 10 kill-time mistakes most people do. Take a close look – which ones apply to you?

I am a perfectionist

I can't even think of doing anything less than perfect and hence, it takes me ages to perfect everything right from the top to bottom. Often while focusing on all possible details – important and not important – I get so carried away and worked up that I am useless for the better part of the day.

Solution – Do aim for perfection; that is a good habit. However, draw a line when it comes to the delivery deadline. There is always scope to improve; but letting go in time will free your mind and time to do and achieve more.

I need to be better than everyone, so I belong

I constantly try to outdo my better-performing colleagues and am always engaging in a mental race with them. I feel that if I do any less, I will no longer belong. I put in a lot of effort to always to a little more and/ or better than anyone else – so I feel appreciated.

Solution: Is this low self-esteem? You do not need to do more than anyone to belong. If at all, you should do it for yourself, for your satisfaction. Focus in giving it your best shot and resist any type of comparison.

I tend to procrastinate

I tend to put off things until the last moment and then I rush through everything at breakneck speed, which often affects the quality of the work. I feel stressed all the time and get less and less done.

Solution: Watch out for telltale signs that procrastination is becoming a habit with you. If so, take immediate steps to …

To check out the rest of **Time Management: The 24.5 hour Day** type the following link into your web browser: http://amzn.to/1NujVjn

Other Books by this Author

For more great titles written by Hanif Raah simply type in the following links into your web browser or search the author account.

Time Management: The 24.5 Hour day

Learn the Skills and Tips on How to Increase Productivity, Save Time, Organize Your Life and Reach Your Goals NOW!

http://amzn.to/1NujVjn

Body Language 101

Discover the Psychology Secrets of How to Read and Understand Non-Verbal Communication and Always Be One Move Ahead

http://amzn.to/1Q7Pcc9

Persuasion: The Subtle Art

How to Influence People to Always Get YOUR Way and
What YOU Want

http://amzn.to/1OnXOJo

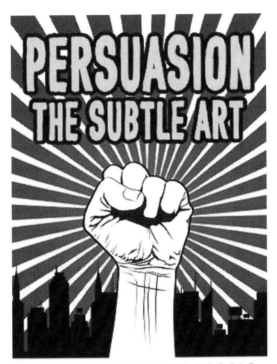

Anger Management

Simple Steps on How to Control Your Temper, Overcome Anger and Start Improving Your Relationships Now!

http://amzn.to/1HpLUQu

Procrastination

A Self Help Cure to Get Things Done, Build Motivation and Break Lazy Habits for Life

http://amzn.to/1AoNpLx

Made in the USA
Middletown, DE
23 December 2016